SEVEN SEAS GHOST SHIP PRESENTS

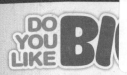

story and art by **GORO AIZOME**

VOLUME 4

TRANSLATION
Miki Z

ADAPTATION
Brett Hallahan

LETTERING
Joven Voon

COVER DESIGN
Nicky Lim

LOGO DESIGN
George Panella

COPY EDITOR
B. Lillian Martin

PROOFREADER
Tui Head

EDITOR
Nick Mamatas

PRODUCTION DESIGNER
George Panella

PRODUCTION MANAGER
Lissa Pattillo

PREPRESS TECHNICIAN
Melanie Ujimori

PRINT MANAGER
Rhiannon Rasmussen-Silverstein

EDITOR-IN-CHIEF
Julie Davis

ASSOCIATE PUBLISHER
Adam Arnold

PUBLISHER
Jason DeAngelis

//// READING DIRECTIONS ////

This book reads from *right to left*,
Japanese style. If this is your first time
reading manga, you start reading from
the top right panel on each page and
take it from there. If you get lost, just
follow the numbered diagram here.
It may seem backwards at first,
but you'll get the hang of it! Have fun!!

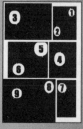

Follow us online: www.GhostShipManga.com

DO YOU LIKE BIG GIRLS?

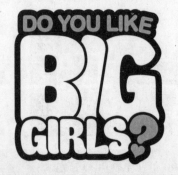

Part Four!

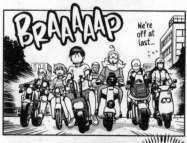

We're off at last...

LOOK!

LET'S ENJOY OUR RIDE, AND THEN WE'LL PRACTICE!

HUH? BUT I WANNA STOP BY THE CAFETERIA!

I COULD GO FOR SOME TAISHO NIKU FRIED RICE*!

I'LL TAKE A NUMBER TEN!

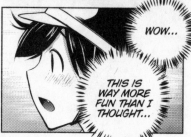

WOW...

THIS IS WAY MORE FUN THAN I THOUGHT...

I CAN TASTE IT NOW!

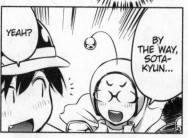

YEAH?

BY THE WAY, SOTA-KYUN...

WE CAN'T STOP! WE GOTTA RIDE THAT BIG WAVE**!

IS THAT EVEN SOMETHING WE CAN RIDE?

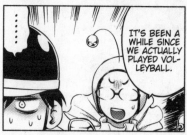

IT'S BEEN A WHILE SINCE WE ACTUALLY PLAYED VOL- LEYBALL.

I'M GREAT WITH MY BOOBS, TOO!
HEY!
YANK

YEP. LIKE I SAID, BEING HORNY.
AND BOOBS AREN'T A SKILL.
I KNOW THAT!
I JUST THOUGHT IT WOULD BE FUNNY.

Part Three!

DON'T WE NEED LI-CENSES?
NOT AS LONG AS WE STAY ON CAMPUS.
Release the clutch slowly...
L-like this?
Yep.
WHOA!
THAT BIKE COST MONEY!
VROOOM
WHAT A DUNCE!
Hahaha!
ONLY GOOD AT VOLLEYBALL AND BEING HORNY!
VRRM
VRRM
GRR!

Part Two!

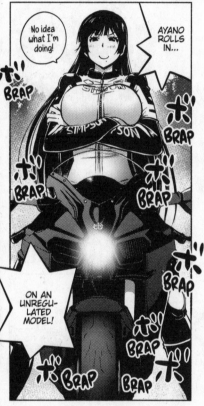

No idea what I'm doing!

AYANO ROLLS IN...

ON AN UNREGULATED MODEL!

BRAP BRAP BRAP BRAP BRAP BRAP

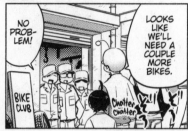

NO PROBLEM!

LOOKS LIKE WE'LL NEED A COUPLE MORE BIKES.

BIKE CLUB

Chatter Chatter

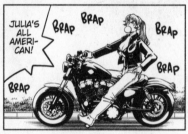

JULIA'S ALL AMERICAN!

BRAP BRAP BRAP BRAP BRAP

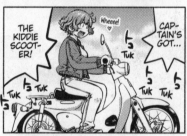

THE KIDDIE SCOOTER!

Wheeee! ♥

CAPTAIN'S GOT...

Tuk Tuk Tuk Tuk Tuk

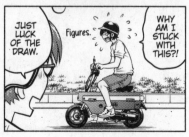

JUST LUCK OF THE DRAW.

Figures.

WHY AM I STUCK WITH THIS?!

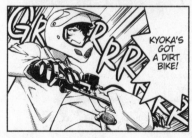

GRRRRR

KYOKA'S GOT A DIRT BIKE!

Bonus Chapter
Amazonians!
Part One!
Squeak
BRAP
BRAP
BRAP
WHAT'S WITH THE BIKE, NEECHAN?
WELL, SEE.
SAKURA MENTIONED BECOMING THE WIND.
SO WE BOR-ROWED IT.
BRAP
BRAP
BRAP
BRAP
THE WIND?
What the heck?
Beats me.
SHE KEEPS TALKING ABOUT "RIDING THAT BIG WAVE."
Vrrrrrr
LET'S GO!!
SA-KURA-SAN?
RIDE OR DIE!

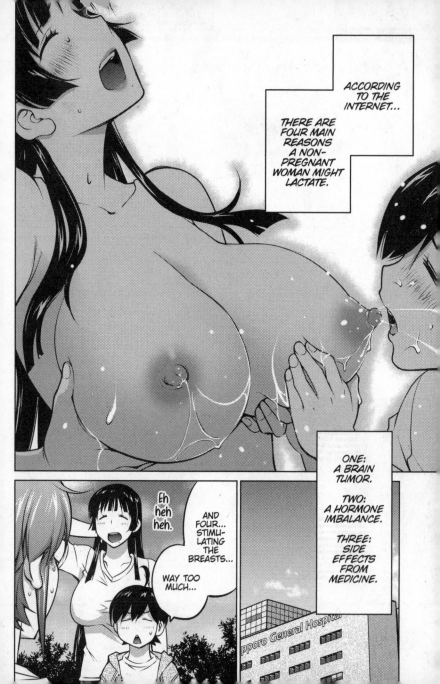

ACCORDING TO THE INTERNET...

THERE ARE FOUR MAIN REASONS A NON-PREGNANT WOMAN MIGHT LACTATE.

ONE: A BRAIN TUMOR.

TWO: A HORMONE IMBALANCE.

THREE: SIDE EFFECTS FROM MEDICINE.

Eh heh heh.

AND FOUR... STIMU-LATING THE BREASTS...

WAY TOO MUCH...

OH!
Spurt
OOPSIE! A LITTLE MILK CAME OUT.
WHAAAT?! WHAT THE HELL WAS THAT?!
IT'S JUST MILK.
YOU DON'T LEAK SOME-TIMES?
NO, I DON'T!!!!
AH!
Shlrrrrp
Shlrrrrrrrp
THAT'S SOME GRIP!

……!!!
WHAT THE HELL KIND OF TORTURE IS THIS?!
Gssssssss!
Throb
Throb
♡
Suck
Suck
Suck
Suck

ちゅぱ Suck
Suck ちゅぱ
Suck ちゅぱ
Suck ちゅぱ
ちゅぱ Suck
Suck ちゅぱ
ちゅぱ Suck
ちゅぱ Suck
ちゅぱ Suck
ちゅぱ Suck
ちゅぱ Suck
ちゅぱ Suck
RGH!
I'M DYING HERE...
THROB
THROB
はっ
GASP!
NO! IT'S NOT WHAT YOU THINK!
I JUST--
NEED TO SIT DOWN!
YOUR NIPPLES SAY DIFFER-ENT...
Heh.
Heh.
I SAID I JUST NEED A BREATH-ER!!!

NEXT!
わっ
Grr!?
AYANO!!!
HERE!
ENJOY!
ぽよん
Jiggle

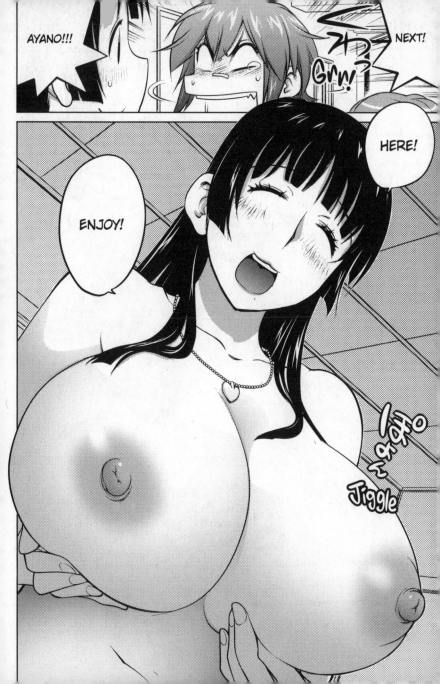

I PREFER IT THIS WAY.
ず GRIND ん
......!
......!!
OH...
Rub
Rub
Rub
MMM!
DIS-QUALI-FIED!
Ker-chak
ガチャ
Tsk!
GET OUT!

Rub
もみ
Rub
もみ
もみ
Rub
もみ
もみ
Rub
Rub
もみ
Rub
もみ
Rub
もみ
Rub
もみ
もみ
Rub
Rub
もみ
Rub
もめ
Rub
もみ
Rub
もみ
Rub
もみ
Rub
もみ
Rub
もみ
Rub
SUUUUUUCK
ちゅううううう
TIME'S UP!!
むははははは
Mwa ha ha ha ha ha!
Snooont
Snoooooont
TIME'S UP! TIME'S UP!!!

Pwip
Ken-Chak
TIME'S UP!
NEXT!

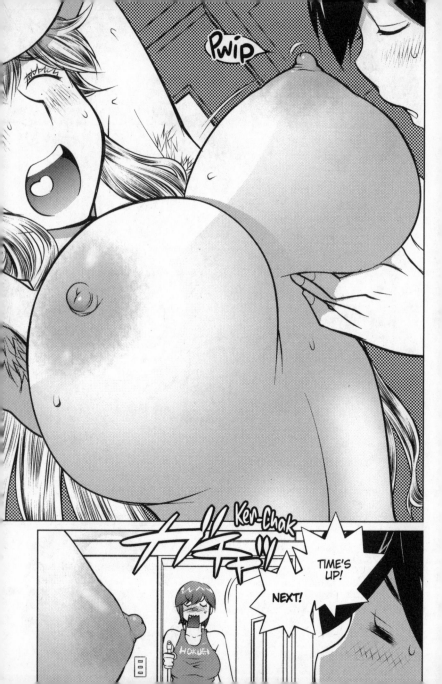

READY! SET! GO!!!
Yahoooo!♥
SHLP
ちゅう Suck
ちゅう Suck
ちゅう Suck
ちゅう Suck
Suck ちゅう

......
Already in position...
......!!
O...
ONLY TEN MINUTES EACH!
わ——い
wheeee!
SHOVE
FIVE MINUTES PER BOOB!
THAT'S ALL YOU GET!!

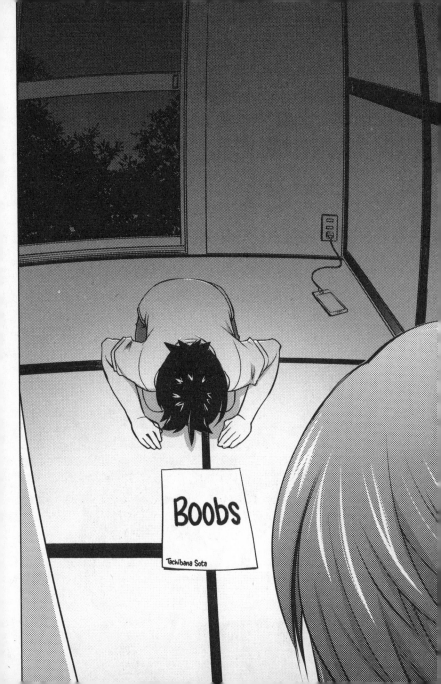

Boobs

Tachibana Sota

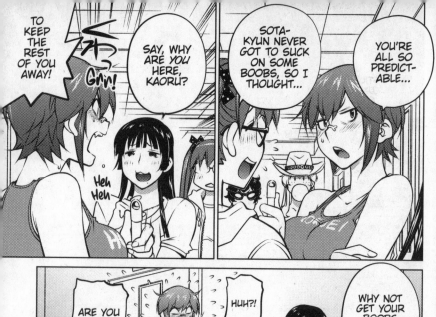

TO KEEP THE REST OF YOU AWAY!

Gr쩌!

SAY, WHY ARE *YOU* HERE, KAORU?

Heh Heh

SOTA-KYUN NEVER GOT TO SUCK ON SOME BOOBS, SO I THOUGHT...

YOU'RE ALL SO PREDICT-ABLE...

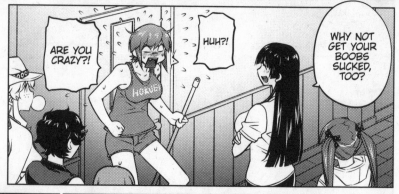

ARE YOU CRAZY?!

HUH?!

WHY NOT GET YOUR BOOBS SUCKED, TOO?

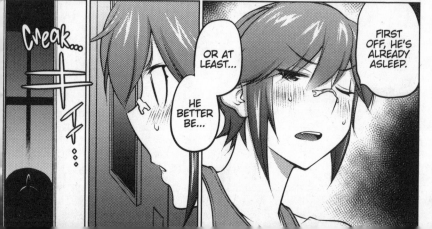

Creak...

OR AT LEAST...

HE BETTER BE...

FIRST OFF, HE'S ALREADY ASLEEP.

BREAK IT UP! BREAK IT UP!
TIME FOR BED! I MEAN IT!
HUH?
BUT MY BOOB...I MEAN MY PHYSICAL THERAPY ISN'T...
I'M DONE.
DEATH!
STILL CHUNKY, EH, CAPTAIN?
GET LOST!
ペタン…
Tip...
パタン…
Toe...
WHAM
ばったり
anitor's Office
……

SHINES THROUGH HER REAR END.
B-U-T-T! SHE MEANS HER BUTT!
するっ
Sfwp
FOR ME, IT'S BOOBS ALL THE WAY.
STOP IGNORING ME!
You're not even looking!
I CAN'T HELP IT WHEN THERE'S BOOBS IN MY FACE!
THEY'RE SOFT AND WARM...
OH!
IT'S LIKE WHEN YOU STICK YOUR HEAD OUT THE WINDOW OF A SPEEDING CAR...
ぐいっ
YANK
IF YOU DON'T SHUT UP ABOUT BOOBS RIGHT NOW...
I WILL KILL YOU.
O... OKAY!

THERE'S NO NEED FOR THAT.
AN INVERTED NIPPLE IS A STATUS SYMBOL.
YOU SHOULD LEAVE IT THE WAY IT IS.
TH... THAT'S RIGHT!
IT'S CUTE!
OH MY GOD.
BOOBS REALLY ARE YOUR FETISH, HUH?
Sigh.
TURN
A GIRL'S REAL CHARM...

STOP!
HEY!!
ENSURING MY TEAM'S GOOD HEALTH IS PART OF MY DUTIES AS COACH.
THAT HAS NOTHING TO DO WITH HER NIPPLES!!
Serious
COME ON, SOTA, LET'S DITCH THESE ANNOYING JERKS.
WHA ?!
HOW DARE YOU!!!
DRAAAG
SLAM

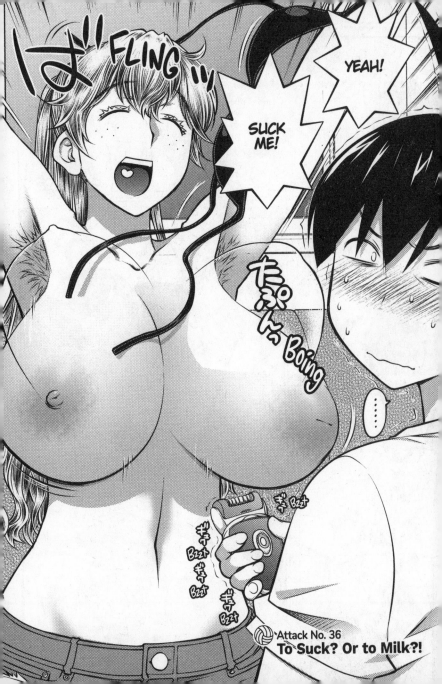

Attack No. 36
To Suck? Or to Milk?!

Bzzt
Bzzt
Bzzt
Bzzt
ssolee
HOW DID I END UP IN CHARGE OF HAIR CARE?
OUCH!
OUCH!
SNIP
Bzzt
SNIP
Bzzt
SNIP
Bzzt
BY THE WAY, JULIA...
YOUR INVERTED NIPPLE.
I BET A GOOD SUCK WOULD POP IT OUT.
...

FARE-
WELL.

MY
FIRST
LOVE.

PSSSSH

PSSSSH

OF
COURSE
NOT!

NEGA-
TIVE!

DON'T
TELL ME
YOU'VE BEEN
HOLDING
IT IN THIS
ENTIRE
TIME?

HUH?

AFTER
THAT, SHE
LOCKED
HERSELF IN
HER ROOM
FOR AN
ENTIRE
WEEK.

Huff!
はぁっ
はぁ、
Huff!
PSSSSH
PSSSSH
Quiver
ぶる、
ぶる、
Quiver

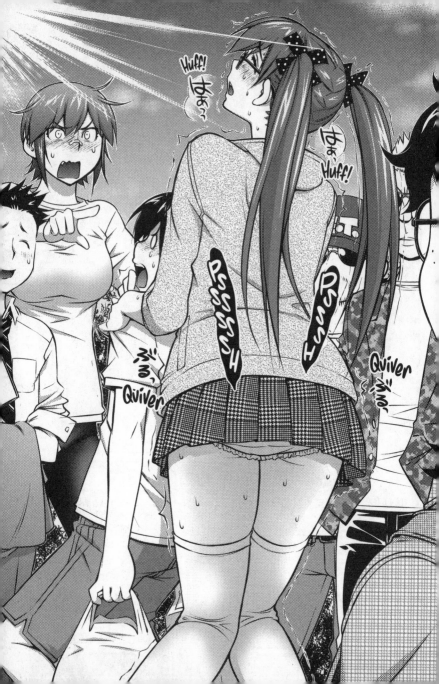

OH.
HI, ASAKURA-SAN'S BOY-FRIEND.
Tremble
UH... UM...
B- BOY-FRIEND?! WHAT ARE YOU TALKING ABOUT?!
Tremble
I CAN'T DO IT.
Huff!
はぁ、
Huff!
はぁ、
Huff!
はぁっ
Huff!
I CAN'T HOLD IT IN ANY-MORE...
IN FRONT OF MY FRIENDS...
AND MY FIRST TRUE LOVE...
Shudder
WIDDLE ME IS...
YOURS TRULY IS...
THIS GIRL HERE IS...
I'M GONNA--

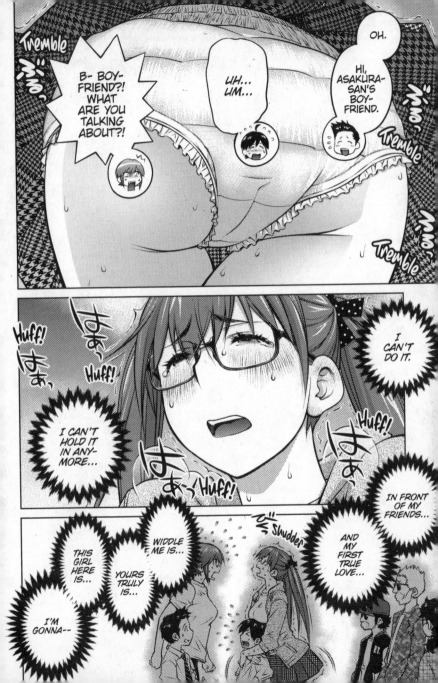

EEP!
Tremble
Tremble
ぎゅっ
Squeeze
WAIT!
squeeeeeeeze
HEY! WHAT'S WITH THE BEAR HUG?!
APRES MOI...
LE DE-LUGE!

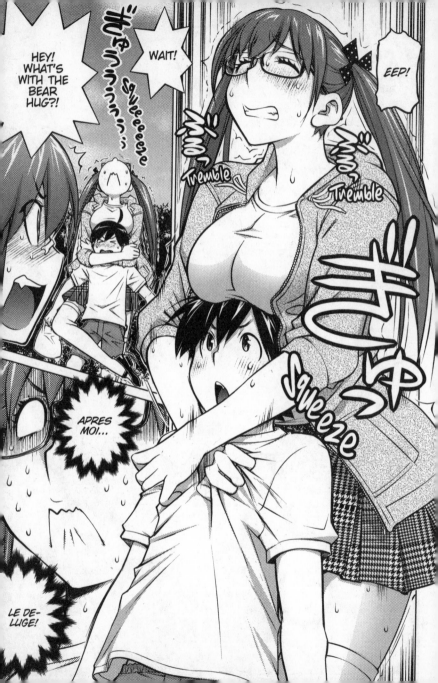

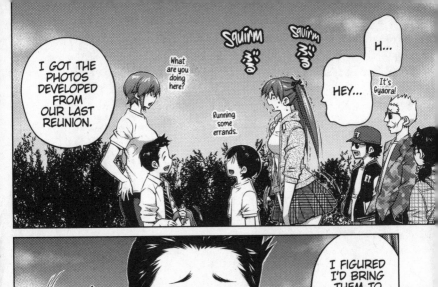

I GOT THE PHOTOS DEVELOPED FROM OUR LAST REUNION.

What are you doing here?

SQUIRM

SQUIRM

H...

HEY...

It's Gyaora!

Running some errands.

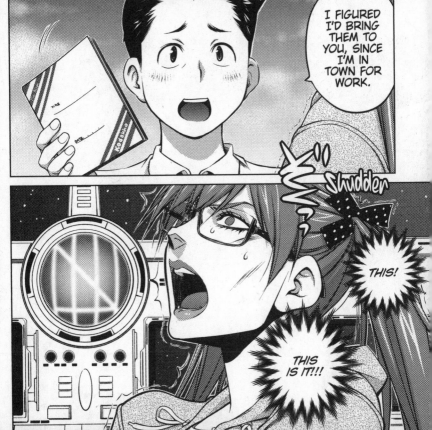

I FIGURED I'D BRING THEM TO YOU, SINCE I'M IN TOWN FOR WORK.

Shudder

THIS!

THIS IS IT!!!

I FINALLY FOUND YOU!
はあ
Huff!
はあ
Huff!
THIS GUY STOPPED BY THE DORM.
APPARENTLY HE CALLS YOU "GIGANTO" OR SOMETHING?
HEY.

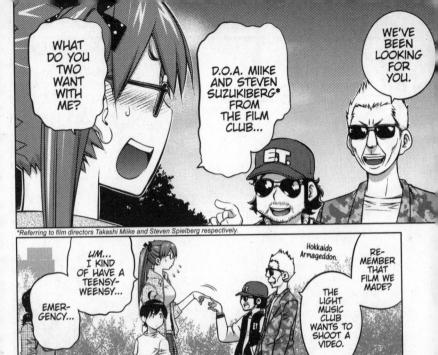

WHAT DO YOU TWO WANT WITH ME?

D.O.A. MIIKE AND STEVEN SUZUKIBERG* FROM THE FILM CLUB...

WE'VE BEEN LOOKING FOR YOU.

*Referring to film directors Takashi Miike and Steven Spielberg respectively.

UM... I KIND OF HAVE A TEENSY-WEENSY...

EMER-GENCY...

Hokkaido Armageddon.

THE LIGHT MUSIC CLUB WANTS TO SHOOT A VIDEO.

RE-MEMBER THAT FILM WE MADE?

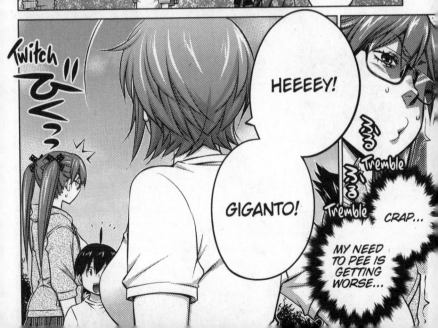

Twitch

HEEEEY!

GIGANTO!

Tremble

Tremble

CRAP...

MY NEED TO PEE IS GETTING WORSE...

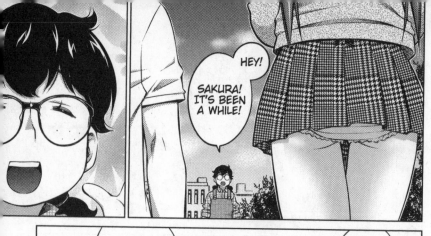

HEY!

SAKURA! IT'S BEEN A WHILE!

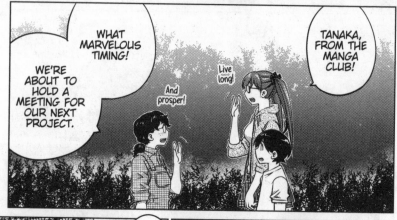

WHAT MARVELOUS TIMING!

WE'RE ABOUT TO HOLD A MEETING FOR OUR NEXT PROJECT.

Live
long!

And
prosper!

TANAKA, FROM THE MANGA CLUB!

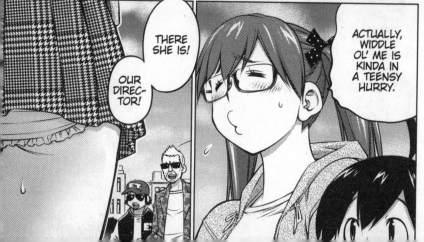

THERE SHE IS!

OUR DIRECTOR!

ACTUALLY, WIDDLE OL' ME IS KINDA IN A TEENSY HURRY.

GO ON.
PEE TO YOUR HEART'S CONTENT.
"How do I look?" she says...
UH... HUH?
SUDDENLY IT'S NOT FEELING SO URGENT.
WHAT?!
I SHOULD BE ABLE TO MAKE IT TO THE BATHROOM.
GREAT...

HOW...
DO I LOOK?
はあ
Huff!
はあ
Huff!

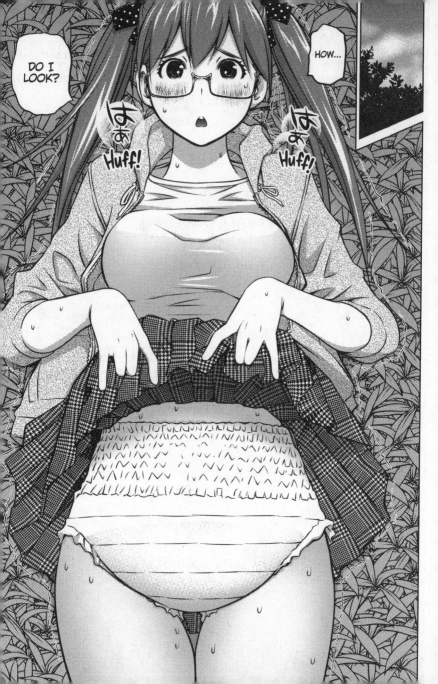

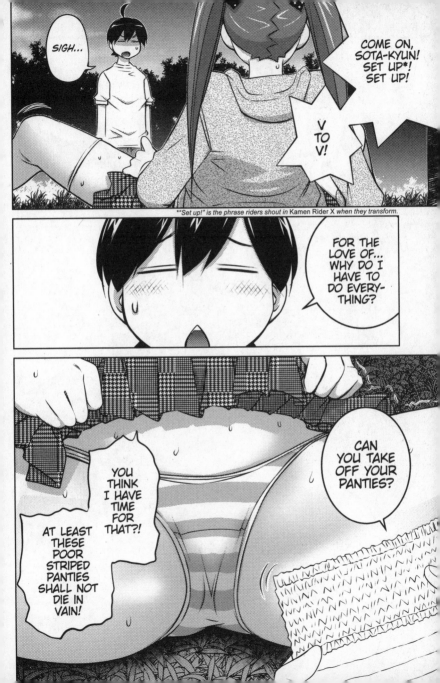

SIGH...

COME ON, SOTA-KYUN! SET UP*! SET UP!

V TO V!

*"Set up!" is the phrase riders shout in Kamen Rider X when they transform.

FOR THE LOVE OF... WHY DO I HAVE TO DO EVERY-THING?

CAN YOU TAKE OFF YOUR PANTIES?

YOU THINK I HAVE TIME FOR THAT?!

AT LEAST THESE POOR STRIPED PANTIES SHALL NOT DIE IN VAIN!

UH...
WHAT ARE YOU DOING?
Grr!
P...
PUT THEM ON ME!!!
Huff!
Huff!
Huff!
AND HERE I THOUGHT I'D NEVER STOOP TO THIS LEVEL OF KINK!!!

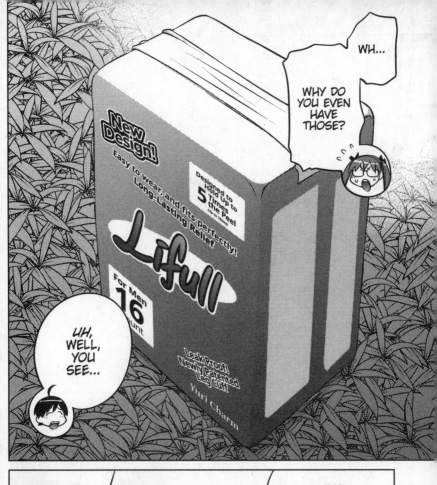

WH...

WHY DO YOU EVEN HAVE THOSE?

New Design!

Easy to wear, and fits perfectly!
Long-Lasting Relief

Designed to Hold Up to 5 Times the Pee! (Up to 18ml)

Lifull

For Men
16 count

Leak Proof!
Newly Patented
Leg cuff!

Yuri Charm

UH, WELL, YOU SEE...

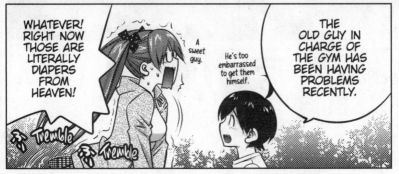

WHATEVER! RIGHT NOW THOSE ARE LITERALLY DIAPERS FROM HEAVEN!

A sweet guy.

He's too embarrassed to get them himself.

THE OLD GUY IN CHARGE OF THE GYM HAS BEEN HAVING PROBLEMS RECENTLY.

Tremble

Tremble

THE SCIENCE LAB NEARBY HAS A BATHROOM.
I WON'T MAKE IT! I CAN'T TAKE ANOTHER STEP!
WHY IS OUR CAMPUS SO SPACIOUS?!
How did you end up in this mess?
I just wanted to go for a walk!
QUIVER
ARGH! I'LL JUST HAVE TO DO IT HERE! SOTA-KYUN, YOU'RE ON GUARD DUTY!
NO WAY!
Shwff
BUT IT'S ILLEGAL!
THIS IS A PRIVATE COLLEGE!
ANYWAY, IT'S RUDE TO PEE IN PUBLIC.
THAT'S WHAT BOTHERS YOU ABOUT THIS?!
OH.
WHY NOT USE THESE?
ADULT DIAPERS.
Fwip
Designed to Hold Up to 5 Times the Pee!
New Design!
Easy to wear, and fits perfectly!
Long-Lasting Relief
BWUH?!

Attack No. 35
First Love ♡ Caught in a Web of Urgency
WHAT ARE YOU DOING BACK THERE?
I GOTTA PEE SO BAD!!
Tremble ぶる
ぶる Tremble
ぶる Tremble
ぶる Tremble
くね Squirm
くね Squirm

MMM!
THE WEATHER'S SO NICE!
くね Squirm
くね Squirm
HRM?
HMM?
SAKURA-SAN...?
Shiver
Shiver
Tremble
ぷる Tremble

ALL RIGHT... LET'S DO IT.

HOKUEI GIRLS!!
NEVER GIVE UP!
YEAAAAAH!

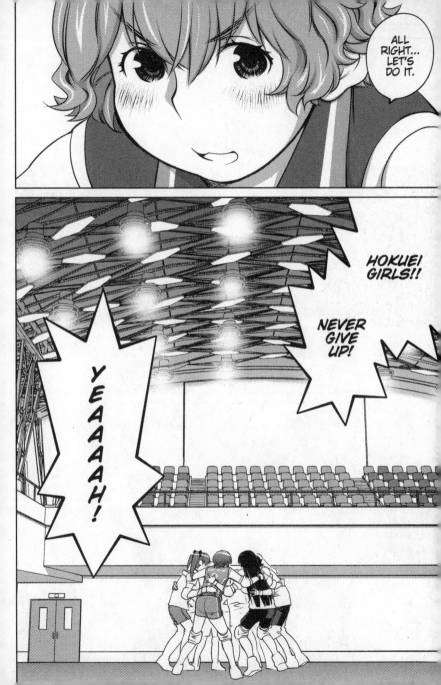

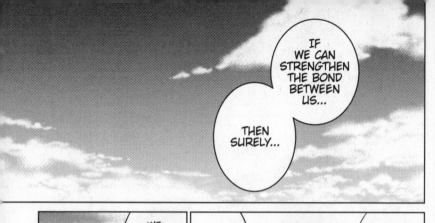

IF WE CAN STRENGTHEN THE BOND BETWEEN US...

THEN SURELY...

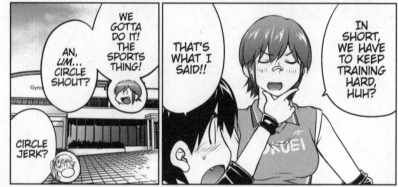

WE GOTTA DO IT! THE SPORTS THING!

AN, UM... CIRCLE SHOUT?

CIRCLE JERK?

THAT'S WHAT I SAID!!

IN SHORT, WE HAVE TO KEEP TRAINING HARD, HUH?

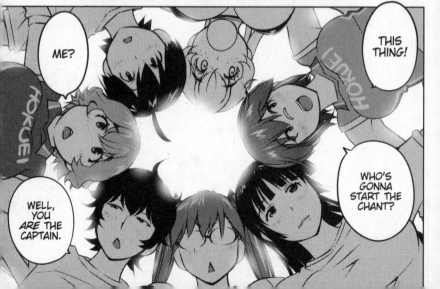

ME?

THIS THING!

WELL, YOU ARE THE CAPTAIN.

WHO'S GONNA START THE CHANT?

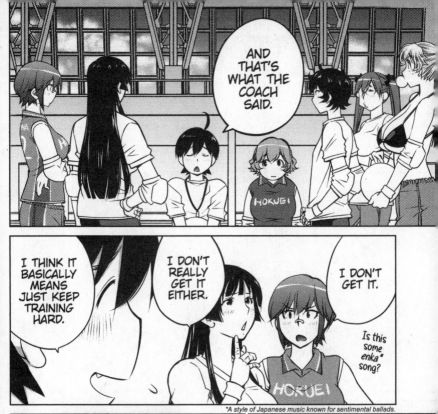

AND THAT'S WHAT THE COACH SAID.

I THINK IT BASICALLY MEANS JUST KEEP TRAINING HARD.

I DON'T REALLY GET IT EITHER.

I DON'T GET IT.

Is this some enka* song?

*A style of Japanese music known for sentimental ballads.

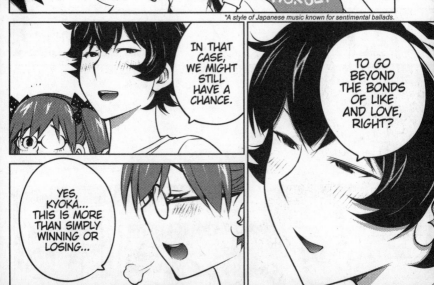

IN THAT CASE, WE MIGHT STILL HAVE A CHANCE.

TO GO BEYOND THE BONDS OF LIKE AND LOVE, RIGHT?

YES, KYOKA... THIS IS MORE THAN SIMPLY WINNING OR LOSING...

UH... SURE.
YOU THREW ME OFF GUARD, GETTING SERIOUS LIKE THAT.
IS IT 'CAUSE YOU'RE GAY?
YOU IDIOT!
I'M BI! BI!
Gymnasium #1

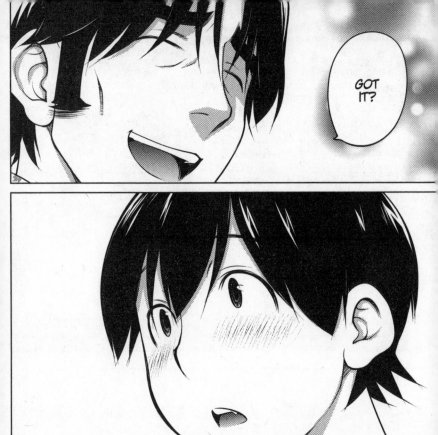

GOT IT?

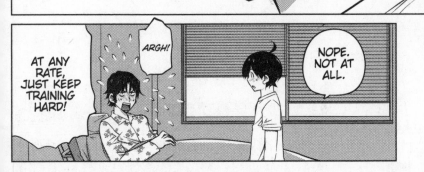

AT ANY RATE, JUST KEEP TRAINING HARD!

ARGH!

NOPE. NOT AT ALL.

THAT, ABOVE ALL ELSE, SHOULD BE YOUR MAIN FOCUS.

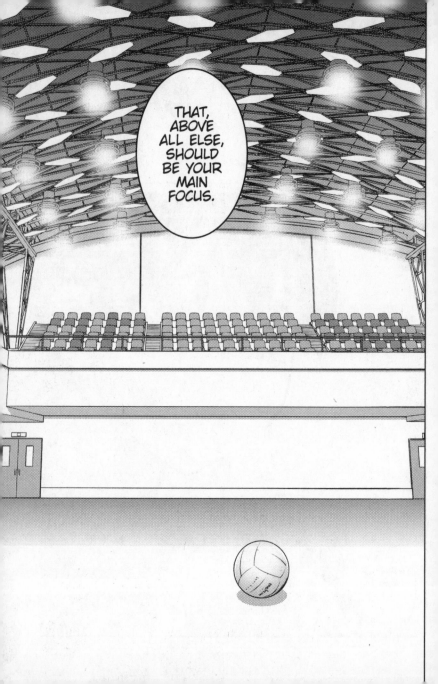

COACHES AND THEIR TEAMS...
TEAM-MATE TO TEAM-MATE...
EVEN BETWEEN RIVALS...
THERE ARE BRIEF MOMENTS WHEN THEIR SOULS ARE CONNECTED.
THIS BOND THAT CONNECTS THEM...
IT GOES BEYOND LOVERS OR EVEN FAMILY.
I NEED YOU TO CARE...
ABOUT NOT JUST SANAE, BUT EVERYONE ON THE TEAM.

THERE'S NO WAY YOU COULD MAKE MY DAUGHTER HAPPY THE WAY YOU ARE NOW.
Huff!
Huff!
I'LL DO...
WHAT-EVER IT TAKES!
I PROMISE TO MAKE HER HAPPY!
IT'S NOT THAT.
LOOK, ATHLETES ARE A DIFFERENT BREED OF PEOPLE.

THEN IT BETTER STAY THAT WAY!
YANK
HUH?
WHAT ...?
WHY?

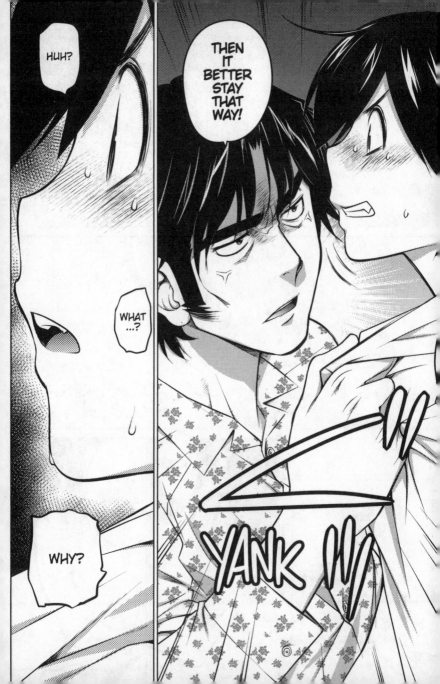

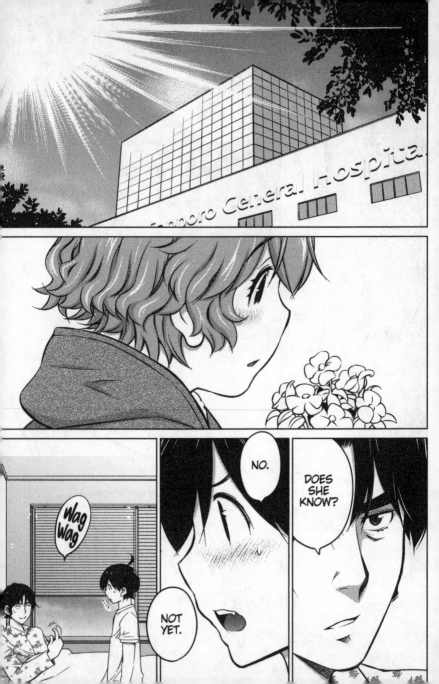

Sapporo General Hospital

WAG WAG

NO.

DOES SHE KNOW?

NOT YET.

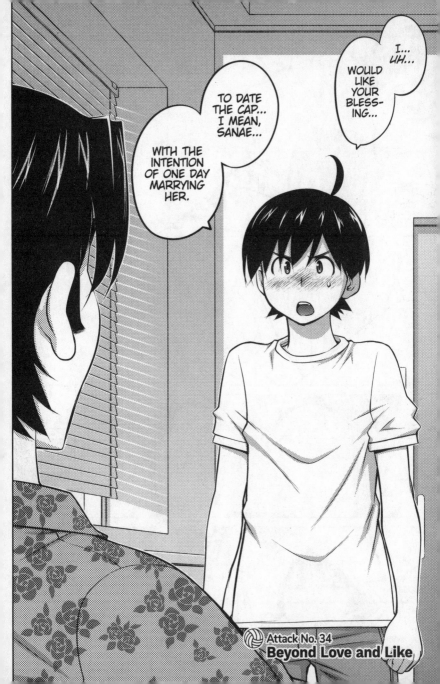

Attack No. 34
Beyond Love and Like

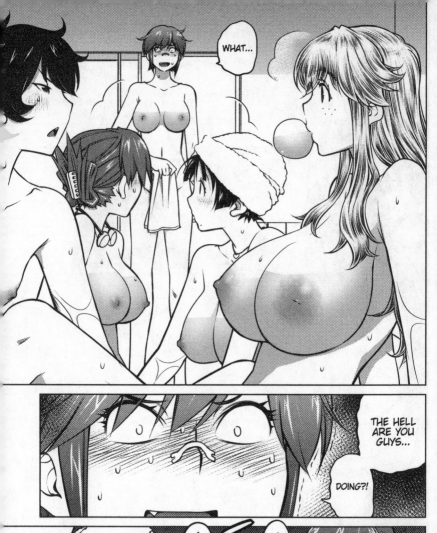

WHAT...

THE HELL
ARE YOU
GUYS...

DOING?!

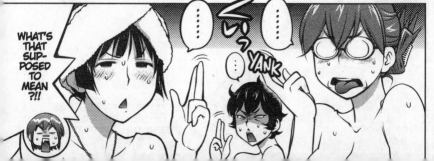

WHAT'S
THAT
SUP-
POSED
TO
MEAN
?!!

......

......

......

YANK

I... UH...
WOULD LIKE YOUR BLESSING...
TO DATE THE CAP... I MEAN, SANAE...
WITH THE INTENTION OF ONE DAY MARRYING HER.

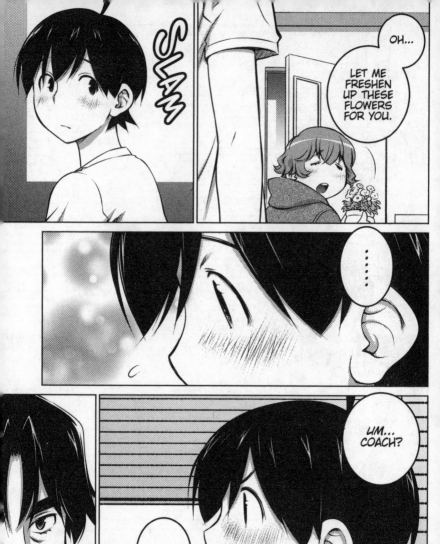

OH...

LET ME FRESHEN UP THESE FLOWERS FOR YOU.

......

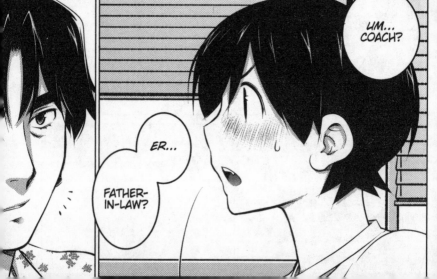

UM... COACH?

ER...

FATHER-IN-LAW?

Hokuei Girls' Dorm Suzuka Villa
WH... WHAT ARE YOU DOING?
......
OF COURSE. STRESS EATING, HUH?
I GET IT, PRINCESS.
BE-CAUSE YOU'RE GAY?
BE-CAUSE I'M *BI*!

UH...

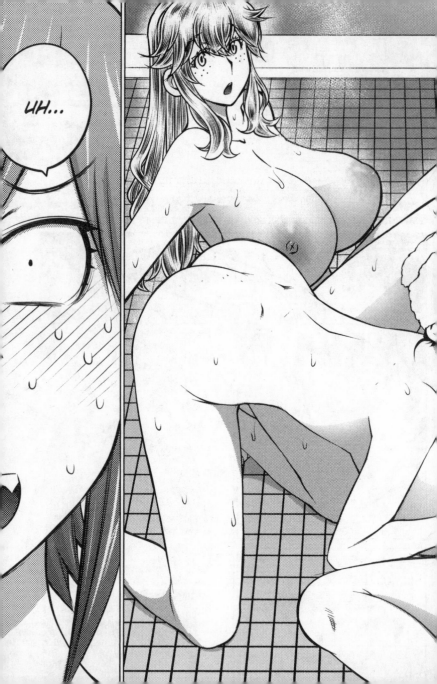

WOW, JULIA...
HOW DOES AYANO HAVE THE TIGHTEST PUSSY OF ALL OF US?
IT'S IMPOS-SIBLE!
ガラッ
Rattle

U-UM!
TH-THAT'S A PRETTY TIGHT PUSSY ALL RIGHT!
WAIT, WAIT!
IS THIS GAY?
My fingers are inside her.
ARE WE HAVING SEX?
IS THIS A BIG DEAL?!
MAYBE I'M THE ONE WHO'S LOOSE...
NO WAY.
D-DON'T SPREAD THEM THAT WIDE!
Shudder
Whoa.
I GOTTA STAY IN CHARACTER! TAKE THAT!
Rub
Rub
YAWN!
I feel so refreshed.
HRM?
IS EVERYONE TAKING A BATH?
Splash
Splash
MAYBE I'LL JOIN THEM.

ば
GRAB
SO?
DOES THIS FEEL LOOSE TO YOU?
WAIT!
HUH?
I JUST MEANT--
YANK
Shlrp

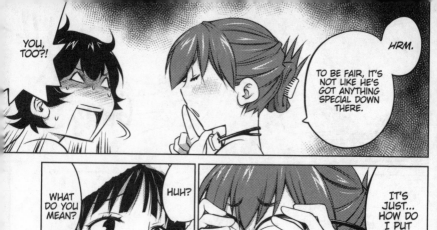

YOU, TOO?!

HRM.

TO BE FAIR, IT'S NOT LIKE HE'S GOT ANYTHING SPECIAL DOWN THERE.

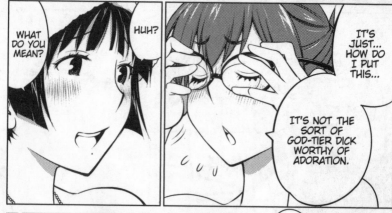

WHAT DO YOU MEAN?

HUH?

IT'S JUST... HOW DO I PUT THIS...

IT'S NOT THE SORT OF GOD-TIER DICK WORTHY OF ADORATION.

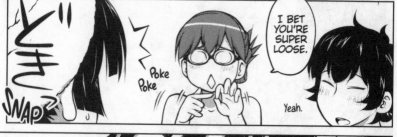

ど ゙ す

SNAP

Poke Poke

I BET YOU'RE SUPER LOOSE.

Yeah.

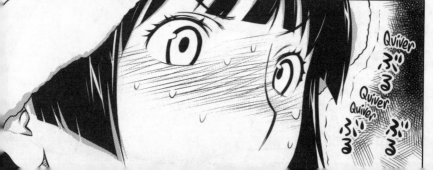

Quiver
ぶ る る

Quiver
ぶ る る

Quiver
ぶ る る

I DUNNO.
I REALLY DO LOVE... HIS DICK.
NO ONE ASKED YOU!
Grr!

Attack No. 33
A Discourse on Tightness

THE WORD "LOVE"...
IT CAN MEAN BOTH LOVE AND LIKE.
WE LIKE SOTA...
BUT SOTA AND KAO-RU...
THEY LOVE EACH OTHER, RIGHT?

I LOVE SOTA-KUN, TOO.
WELL, HIS DICK, AT LEAST.
WHAT ARE WE GONNA DO WITH YOU...
むにゃ Nyam
むにゃ Nyam

SOTA-KYUN LOVES THE CAPTAIN...
OR AT LEAST, THAT'S WHAT HE THINKS.
IN FACT, HE ACTUALLY LOVES KAORU THE MOST.
AND KAORU LOOOVES HER LITTLE BROTHER, SOTA.
A FOR-BIDDEN LOVE AFFAIR.
WE'RE NOTHING BUT BIT PLAYERS IN THE BACK-GROUND.
WE ARE?
WE ARE.
I GUESS SO.
AND YOU ...?
RIGHT. WHAT DOES THE HORNY BEAST CARE?
HORNY BEAST? SOUNDS KINKY!

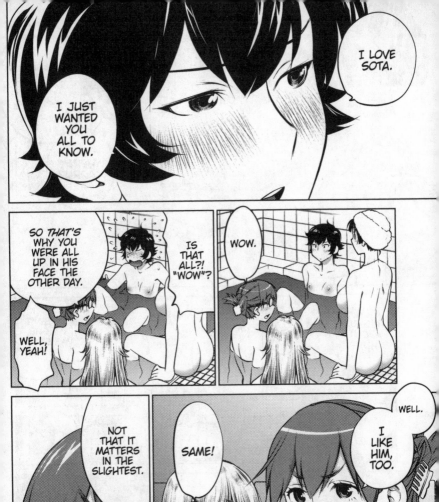

I LOVE SOTA.

I JUST WANTED YOU ALL TO KNOW.

SO *THAT'S* WHY YOU WERE ALL UP IN HIS FACE THE OTHER DAY.

IS THAT ALL?! "WOW"?

WELL, YEAH!

WOW.

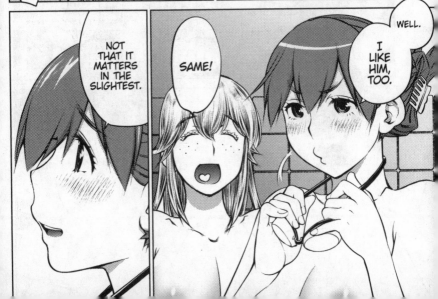

NOT THAT IT MATTERS IN THE SLIGHTEST.

SAME!

WELL. I LIKE HIM, TOO.

WELL... I GUESS YOU CAN JOIN US.
WHERE'S KAORU?
ISN'T SHE STILL ASLEEP?
WHY? WHAT'S UP?
WHAT'S THIS ALL ABOUT, HUH?
DUNNO.
KYOKA'S THE ONE WHO WOKE US ALL UP.
LOOK...
I'VE BEEN THINKING ABOUT THIS FOR A WHILE.
I REALIZED SOME-THING.

Bathroom
RATTLE
WHY'S EVERYONE TAKING A MORNING BATH?
AYANO?

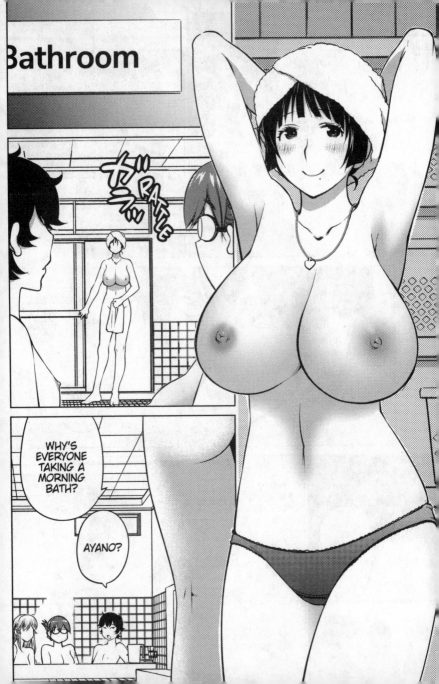

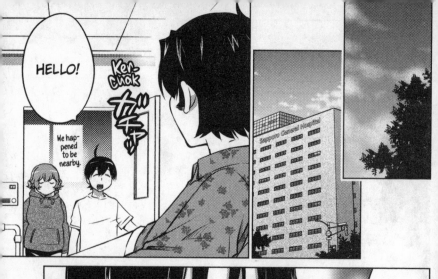

HELLO!

Ker-chak

We happened to be nearby.

Sapporo General Hospital

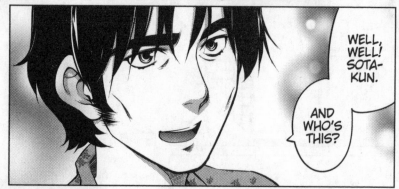

WELL, WELL! SOTA-KUN.

AND WHO'S THIS?

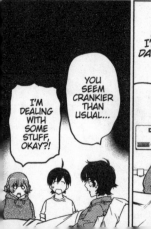

I'M DEALING WITH SOME STUFF, OKAY?!

YOU SEEM CRANKIER THAN USUAL...

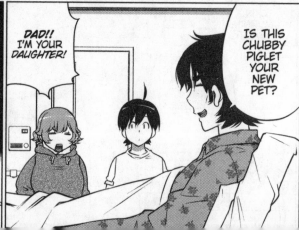

DAD!! I'M YOUR DAUGHTER!

IS THIS CHUBBY PIGLET YOUR NEW PET?

......! ......!
GRIND
GRIND
FOR CRYING OUT LOUD... SHE'S ALWAYS ON YOUR MIND, HUH?
GRIND
GRIND
GRIND
...!!! !!!

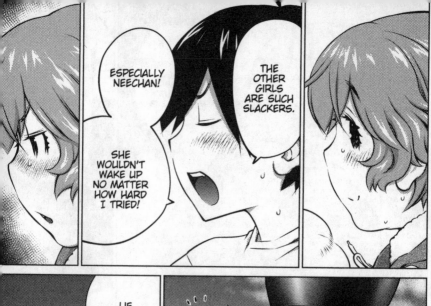

THE OTHER GIRLS ARE SUCH SLACKERS.

ESPECIALLY NEECHAN!

SHE WOULDN'T WAKE UP NO MATTER HOW HARD I TRIED!

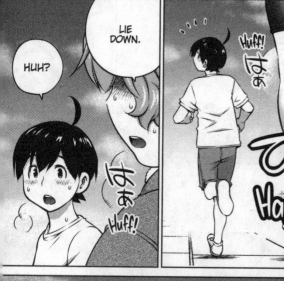

HUH?

LIE DOWN.

はぁ Huff!

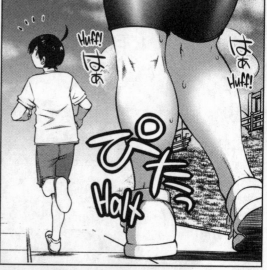

Huff! はぁ

はぁ Huff!

ぴたっ Halt

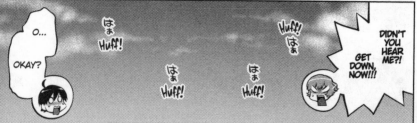

O...

OKAY?

はぁ Huff!

はぁ Huff!

はぁ Huff!

はぁ Huff!

DIDN'T YOU HEAR ME?! GET DOWN, NOW!!!

Attack No. 32
Play Pig Part II (3)

WELL...
I'M ALWAYS HAPPY FOR SOME QUALITY TIME WITH YOU.
はぁ Huff!
はぁ Huff!
た、Tmp
Tmp た、
た、Tmp

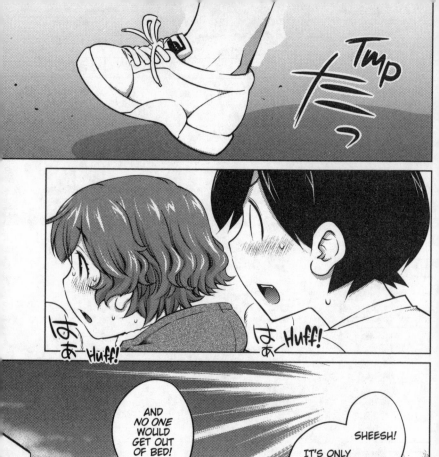

Tmp

Huff!

Huff!

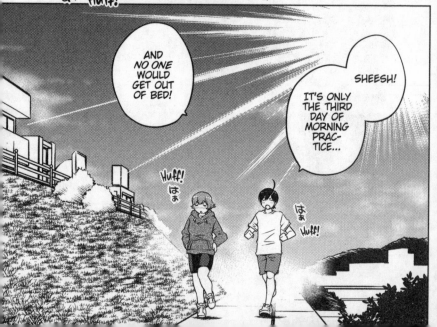

AND NO ONE WOULD GET OUT OF BED!

SHEESH!

IT'S ONLY THE THIRD DAY OF MORNING PRACTICE...

Huff!

Huff!

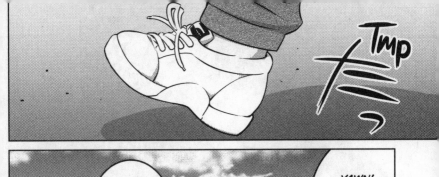

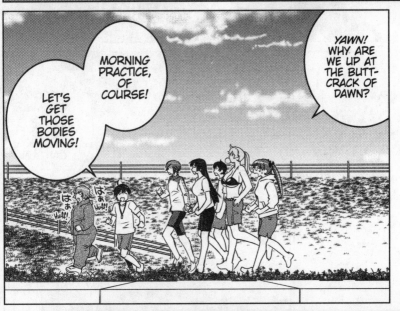

MORNING PRACTICE, OF COURSE!

LET'S GET THOSE BODIES MOVING!

YAWN! WHY ARE WE UP AT THE BUTT-CRACK OF DAWN?

はぁ Huff!!

はぁ Huff!!

はぁ Huff!!

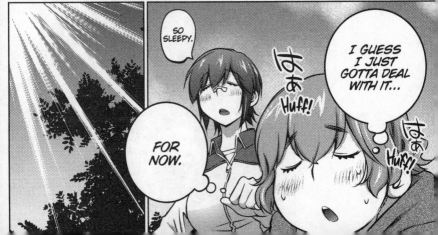

SO SLEEPY.

I GUESS I JUST GOTTA DEAL WITH IT...

FOR NOW.

はぁ Huff!

はぁ Huff!!

......!!
GRIND
GRIND
GRIND
......!!
GRIND
GOOD MORNING. IT'S ME, THE CHUNKY CAPTAIN.
はぁ Huff!
ふぅ wheeze
WANNA...
JOIN ME FOR A JOG?

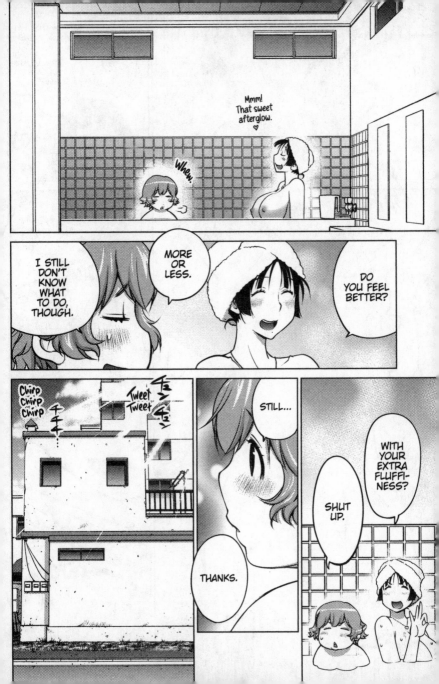

Mmm! That sweet afterglow. ♡

Whew.

I STILL DON'T KNOW WHAT TO DO, THOUGH.

MORE OR LESS.

DO YOU FEEL BETTER?

Chirp Chirp Chirp

Tweet Tweet

STILL...

WITH YOUR EXTRA FLUFFI- NESS?

SHUT UP.

THANKS.

ARE YOU GONNA CUM?
ARE YOU CLOSE?
I WANNA SEE!
Shudder
Huff!
Huff!
Huff!
Huff!
Huff!
Tremble
Ah!
Ah!
Gasp!

MM-HM!
JUST HERE?
SEEMS LIKE THE SPOT!
Huff!
Huff!
Huff!
YOU...
JERK...
Shlk
Shlk
Shlk
DAY
OH!
STOP!
STOP...
THIS?
Shlp
Tremble
DON'T!
Shlk
Shlk
YOUR FINGERS ARE... TOO LONG.
Twitch
Poke
Poke
Poke
T...
TOO DEEP!
Twitch

THEY'RE SIBLINGS.
THEY'VE BEEN TOGETHER FOR MOST OF THEIR LIVES.
DAY BREEZE
NATURAL+AID FOR THE BODY
BODY SHAMPOO
THERE'S NO WAY I CAN BEAT HER...
THOSE TWO REALLY NEED TO FUCK ALREADY.
POOR KAORU.
SHE'S ALWAYS BEEN THAT WAY, THOUGH...
WELL.
WHAT-EVER!
NOW SPREAD THOSE LEGS OF YOURS.
Spread
DAY BREEZE
WH-WHAT...
TH-THAT'S MY...
BODY SHAMPOO

THE PERSON WHO TOLD ME HE LOVES ME...
HE LOVES SOME-ONE ELSE.
YET HE SEEMS COMPLETELY BLIND TO THAT FACT.
IT'S PRETTY FRUS-TRATING.
SOUNDS LIKE IT.

YOU'RE CUTE AND ADOR-ABLE!
ちゅ Kiss
ちゅ Kiss
びくっ Shiver
MMM...
CHEER UP, CAPTAIN!
NO...
Flick Flick
はぁ Huff!
YOU GO AROUND DOING WHATEVER (AND WHOMEVER) YOU LIKE WITHOUT A CARE, HUH?
はぁ Huff!
YEP! PRETTY MUCH.
THAT'S NOT HOW IT WORKS!
もみ Rub
もみ Rub
COME TO PRACTICE AGAIN.
OKAY?

♡
DAY BREEZE
YOU'RE LIKE A SQUISHY LITTLE TEDDY BEAR.
JUST SAY I'M FAT.

Hokuei College Girls' Dorm Suzuka Villa
ARE YOU AWAKE, CAPTAIN? IT'S ME, AYANO.
WANNA JOIN ME FOR A BATH?
Knock Knock
......
WANNA WATCH SOME PORN WITH ME?
It's a new release! ♥
NOT INTER-ESTED!
One-Way Mirror
I'VE GOT A SHORT-BREAD COOKIE WITH YOUR NAME ON IT...
Creak
Bath first, then cookie.
Cookie! Cookie!

BONK
OOF!
AWW!
OUCH! WHAT'S WRONG WITH YOU, NEE-CHAN?!
AWW!
SHUT! THE HELL! UUUP!
AWW!
THOSE TWO ARE A REAL PAIN IN THE BUTT SOMETIMES...

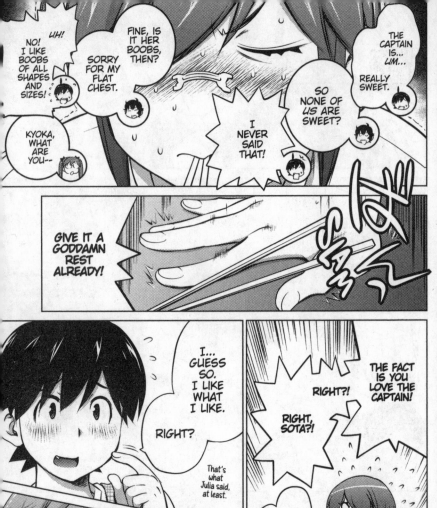

NO! I LIKE BOOBS OF ALL SHAPES AND SIZES!

UH!

SORRY FOR MY FLAT CHEST.

FINE, IS IT HER BOOBS, THEN?

THE CAPTAIN IS... UM...

REALLY SWEET.

KYOKA, WHAT ARE YOU--

I NEVER SAID THAT!

SO NONE OF US ARE SWEET?

GIVE IT A GODDAMN REST ALREADY!

SLAM

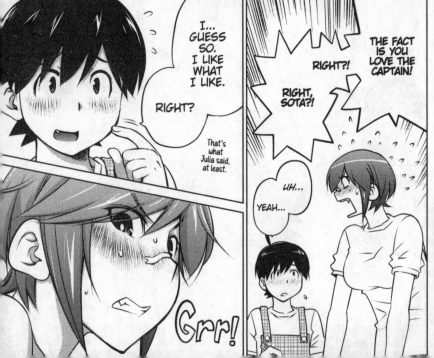

I... GUESS SO. I LIKE WHAT I LIKE.

RIGHT?

That's what Julia said, at least.

THE FACT IS YOU LOVE THE CAPTAIN!

RIGHT?!

RIGHT, SOTA?!

UH... YEAH...

Grr!

TH...
THAT SHE'S SO TINY.
IT SETS HER APART FROM THE REST OF YOU GIANTS.
BUT WASN'T AYANO YOUR FIRST CRUSH?
SHE'S FAR FROM TINY.
THAT WAS...
BEFORE I LEARNED WHAT A PERVERTED FREAK SHE IS.
AWW! YOU'RE SO MEAN!
THEN THERE'S THAT EX OF YOURS.
SHE WAS PRETTY BIG, TOO.
OR RATHER, *THICK*?
SO? NEE-CHAN INTRODUCED US.
OH? REALLY?
YEAH... ONE DAY OUT OF NOWHERE SHE TELLS ME IT'S ABOUT TIME I FOUND A GIRL.

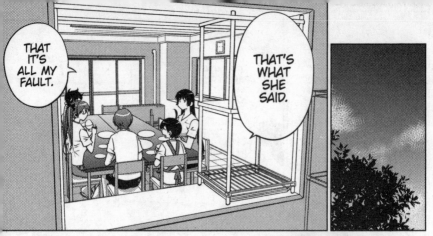

THAT IT'S ALL MY FAULT.

THAT'S WHAT SHE SAID.

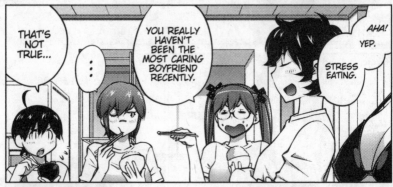

THAT'S NOT TRUE...

...

YOU REALLY HAVEN'T BEEN THE MOST CARING BOYFRIEND RECENTLY.

AHA!

YEP.

STRESS EATING.

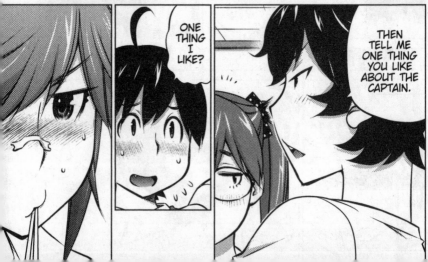

ONE THING I LIKE?

THEN TELL ME ONE THING YOU LIKE ABOUT THE CAPTAIN.

IT'S ALL BE-CAUSE...
YOU DON'T REALLY CARE ABOUT ME AT ALL.

Attack No. 32
Play Pig Part II (2)

Hokuei College Girls' Dorm Suzuka Villa

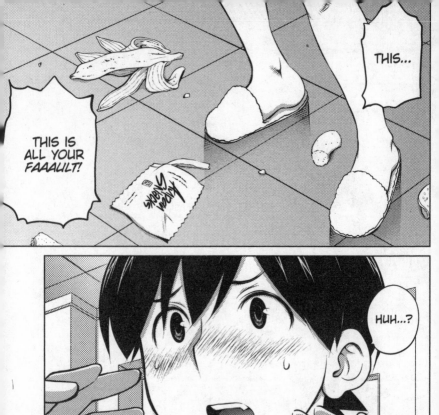

THIS...

THIS IS ALL YOUR FAAAULT!

HUH...?

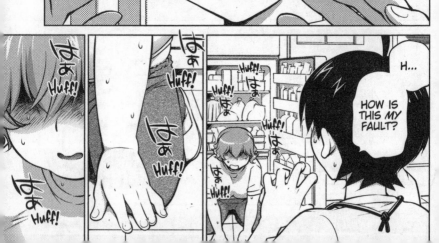

Huff!

Huff!

Huff!

Huff!

Huff!

Huff!

Huff!

H...

HOW IS THIS MY FAULT?

HEY!
ポコ THWAP
SHUT UP!
SHUT UP! SHUT UP!
Rawr!
Rawr!
ポコ THWAP
WHAT'S THE MATTER WITH YOU?!
PLEASE, JUST TALK TO ME...
はあ Huff!
はあ はあ Huff! Huff!
PLIP
THIS...
THIS IS ALL YOUR FAAAULT!

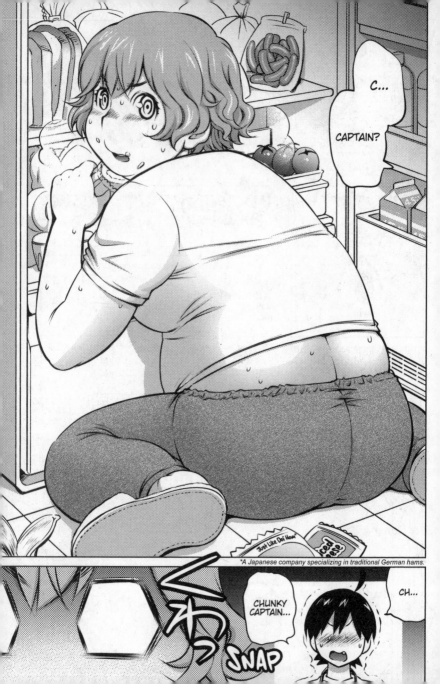

C...

CAPTAIN?

"Just Like Doi Ham"

*A Japanese company specializing in traditional German hams.

CHUNKY CAPTAIN...

CH...

SNAP

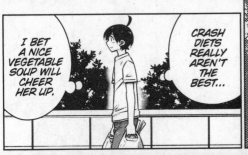

I BET A NICE VEGETABLE SOUP WILL CHEER HER UP.

CRASH DIETS REALLY AREN'T THE BEST...

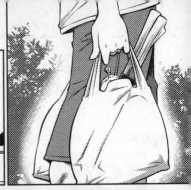

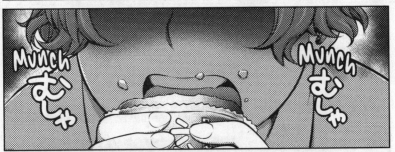

MUNCH むしゃ

MUNCH むしゃ

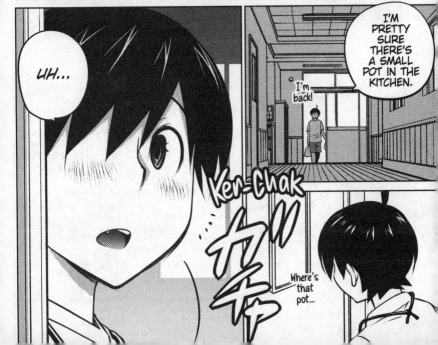

UH...

I'M PRETTY SURE THERE'S A SMALL POT IN THE KITCHEN.

I'm back!

Ker-Chak カラ!! ガチャ

Where's that pot...

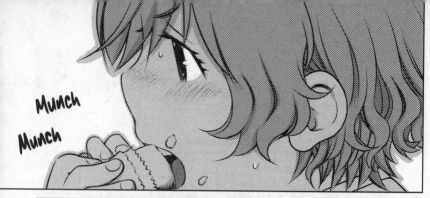

Munch

Munch

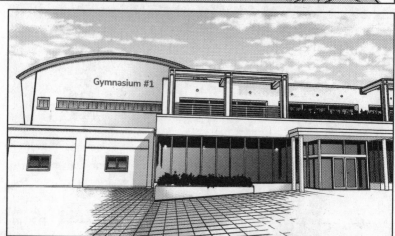

Gymnasium #1

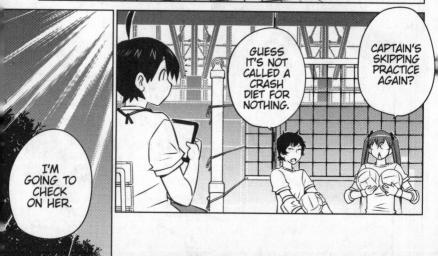

GUESS IT'S NOT CALLED A CRASH DIET FOR NOTHING.

CAPTAIN'S SKIPPING PRACTICE AGAIN?

I'M GOING TO CHECK ON HER.

UH... CAPTAIN?
IT'S DINNER-TIME.
KNOCK
こん
こん
KNOCK
I DON'T WANT ANY.
I'M NOT HUN-GRY.
OH.
OKAY.
CHIPS
THAT'S WHAT SHE SAID.
HONESTLY, SHE COULD STAND TO LOSE A FEW POUNDS.
I CAN'T BELIEVE YOU BASICALLY CALLED HER FAT.

IT'S NO BIG DEAL.
NO PROBLEM AT ALL!
WELL.
THAT'S JUST HOW IT GOES, Y'KNOW?
UM, CAPTAIN?
YOU'VE GAINED WEIGHT, HUH?
GAH!
Hokuei Girls' Dorm Suzuka Villa

ピー
TWEEEET!
Gymnasium #1
GOOD GAME!
YOU TOO!
Locker Room
AWW! CAN'T BELIEVE WE LOST.
Chatter Chatter
ぞろぞろ
LET'S GO GET DINNER!
I'M STARV-ING.
I'M SORRY...
IT'S ALL MY FAULT.
HOKUEI

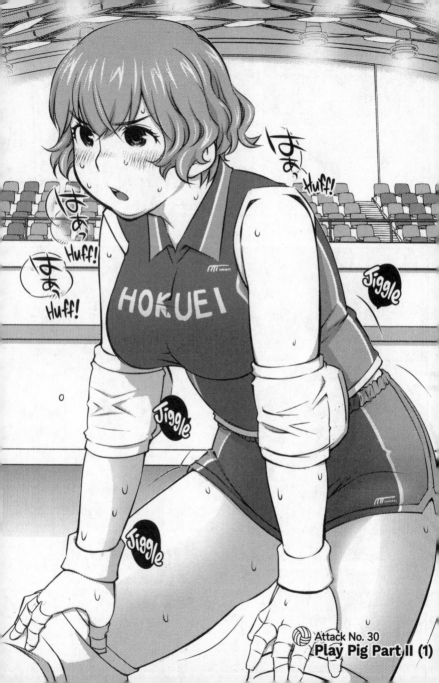

Attack No. 30
Play Pig Part II (1)

DON'T WORRY, CAPTAIN!
はぁ、Huff!
YAMADA
6
SHAKE IT OFF! SHAKE IT OFF!
はぁ、Huff!
はぁ、Huff!
はぁ、Huff!
はぁ、Huff!
CAPTAIN!
BAM

THWAP
WHAM

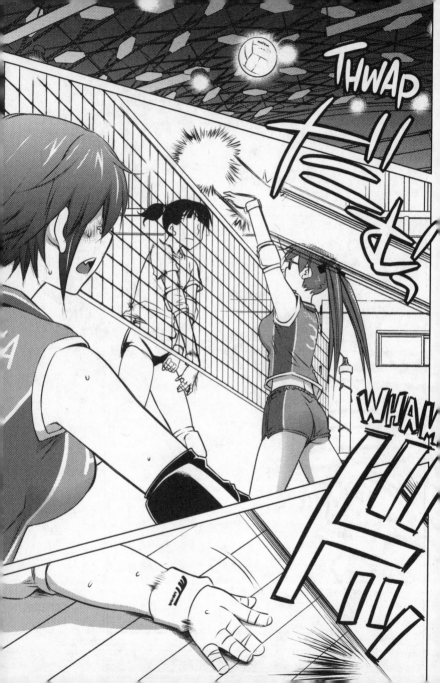

THE MOST MAGNIF-ICENT DICK CLOUD!
WOW! NO KIDDING.
DO YOU EVER GIVE IT A REST?!

I CAN'T BELIEVE...
THEY'VE ALL...
STUCK THAT INSIDE THEM.
I CAN'T... THERE'S ABSOLUTELY NO WAY...
HOKUEI
OH!
CHECK IT OUT!
WHAT'S UP, AYANO?

I'M JUST GLAD SOTA'S FINALLY BACK TO NORMAL.
S...
SORRY FOR WORRYING EVERYONE.
SHEESH.
YEAH!
FEEL FREE TO CALL ME NEECHAN WHENEVER YOU WANT, THOUGH.
ME TOO! ME TOO!
I CAN BE YOUR AMERICAN NEECHAN!
KN...
KNOCK IT OFF!
SIBLINGS DON'T DO THAT KIND OF STUFF!

BANG! THWAP! POW! SLAM!

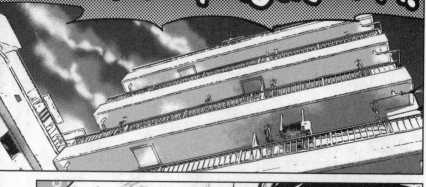

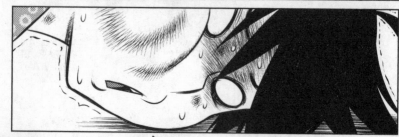

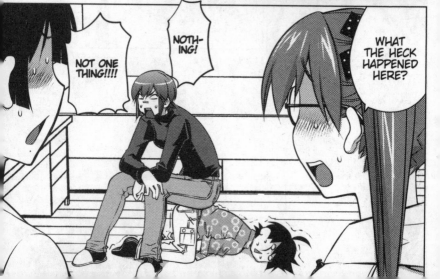

WHAT THE HECK HAPPENED HERE?

NOTH-ING!

NOT ONE THING!!!!

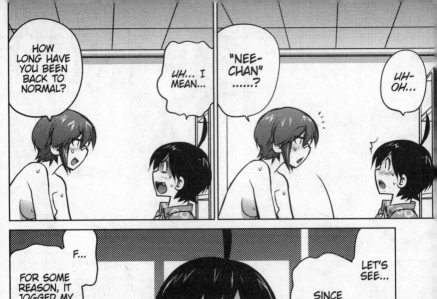

HOW LONG HAVE YOU BEEN BACK TO NORMAL?

UH... I MEAN...

"NEE-CHAN" ......?

UH-OH...

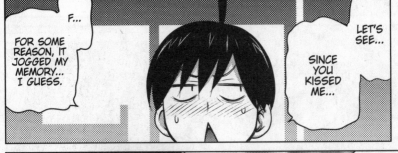

F...

FOR SOME REASON, IT JOGGED MY MEMORY... I GUESS.

LET'S SEE...

SINCE YOU KISSED ME...

FLOATING IN A SEA OF BOOBS WAS SO EUPHORIC...

WHY DIDN'T YOU SAY SOME-THING?!

YOU DON'T HAVE TO...!
WAIT!!!
I SAID STOP, NEECHAN!!!!

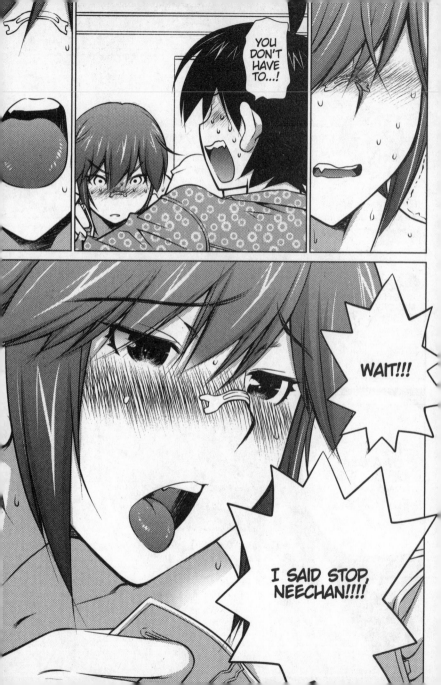

LIE BACK AND LET YOUR NEECHAN TAKE CARE OF IT...
Pull

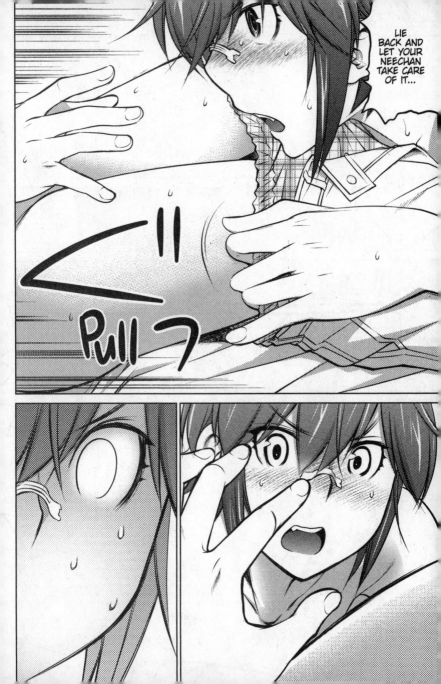

NOW THEN... WHAT NEXT?
WH... WHAT?
YOU WANNA MASSAGE MY BOOBS?
UH... UM...
FORGET IT.
Ziiiip
YOU'RE MY YOUNGER BROTHER!
SO LET ME HANDLE THIS!
HEY!
WAIT!
YANK

Ba-dump
Ba-dump
HEY!
Ba-dump
A... UH--
Ba-dump
KAORU-SAN!
Ba-dump

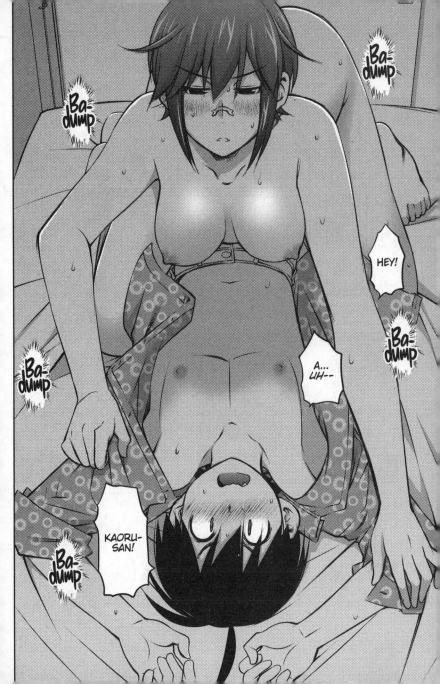

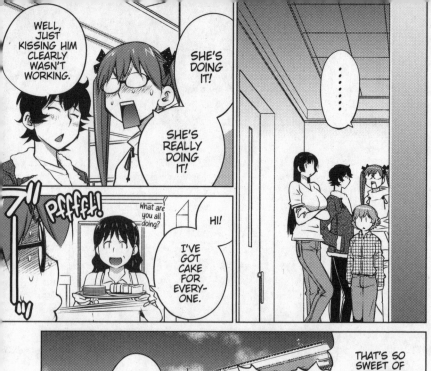

WELL, JUST KISSING HIM CLEARLY WASN'T WORKING.

SHE'S DOING IT!

SHE'S REALLY DOING IT!

PFFFH!

What are you all doing?

HI!

I'VE GOT CAKE FOR EVERYONE.

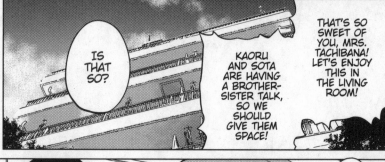

IS THAT SO?

KAORU AND SOTA ARE HAVING A BROTHER-SISTER TALK, SO WE SHOULD GIVE THEM SPACE!

THAT'S SO SWEET OF YOU, MRS. TACHIBANA! LET'S ENJOY THIS IN THE LIVING ROOM!

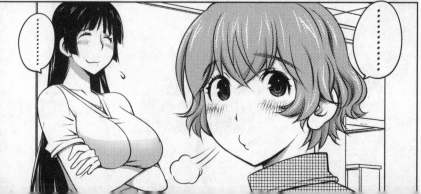

Y-YES...
MA'AM.
Ba-dump
HUFF!
Ba-dump
HUFF!
Ba-dump
Ba-dump
Ba-dump
HUFF!
HUFF!
Ba-dump
Ba-dump

WHA...
B...
BED! NOW!
OKAY!

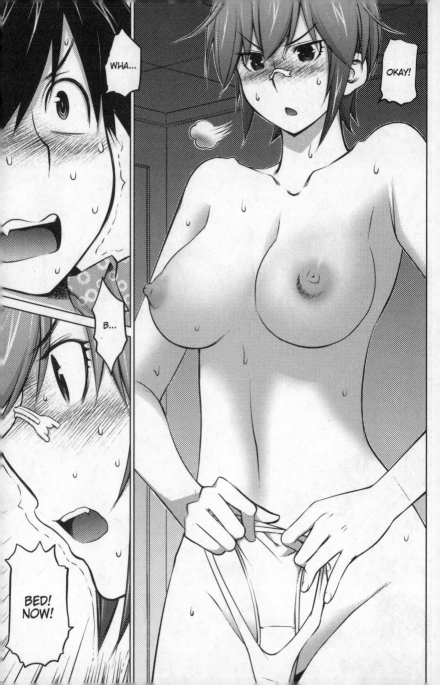

SEE YA!
BEST OF LUCK!
しゅた!
Fwing
WE'RE ROOTING FOR YOU!
......
パタン
SLAM
U-UM...
UH...
するっ
Slide
HEY!!!

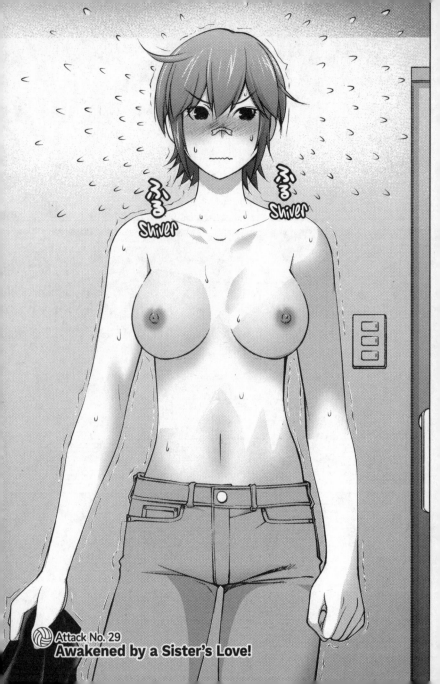

Attack No. 29
Awakened by a Sister's Love!

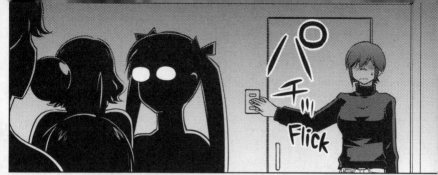

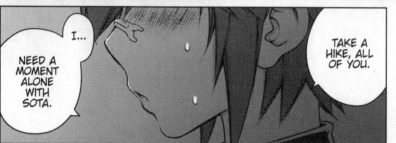

I...

NEED A MOMENT ALONE WITH SOTA.

TAKE A HIKE, ALL OF YOU.

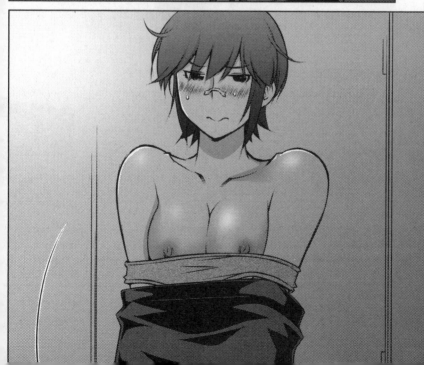

はぁ
Huff!
Huf
はぁ
squish
むにゅ
Huff!
はぁ
はぁ
Huff!
むにゅ
squish
THERE'S SOMETHING I NEED TO REMEMBER, AND IT'S RIGHT ON THE TIP OF MY TONGUE...
はぁ
Huff!
はぁ
Huff!

SIGH...
WOW...
Huff! はぁ
IT'S LIKE...
はぁ Huff!
Huff! はぁ
むにゅ Squish
はぁ Huff!
はぁ Huff!
むにゅ Squish

C'MON...
YOU GUYS...
WHAT ARE YOU...

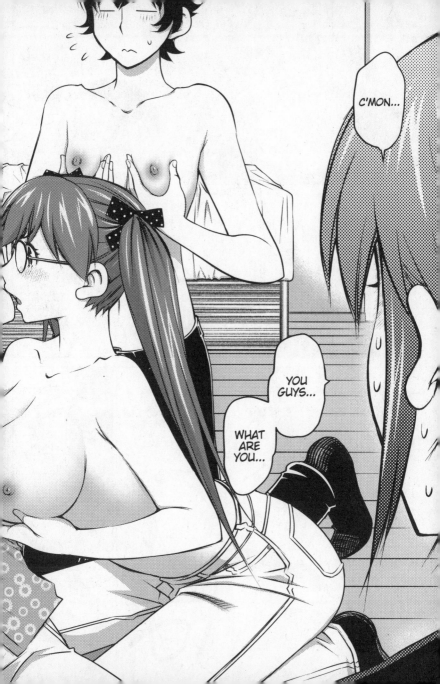

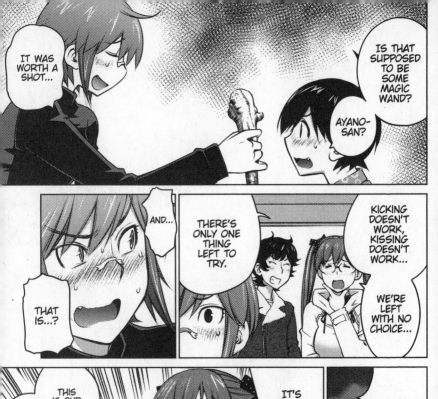

IT WAS WORTH A SHOT...

IS THAT SUPPOSED TO BE SOME MAGIC WAND?

AYANO-SAN?

AND...

THERE'S ONLY ONE THING LEFT TO TRY.

KICKING DOESN'T WORK, KISSING DOESN'T WORK...

WE'RE LEFT WITH NO CHOICE...

THAT IS...?

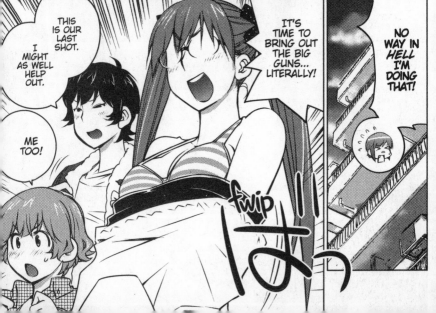

THIS IS OUR LAST SHOT.

I MIGHT AS WELL HELP OUT.

IT'S TIME TO BRING OUT THE BIG GUNS... LITERALLY!

NO WAY IN *HELL* I'M DOING THAT!

ME TOO!

fwip

GOT IT!
WHAT'S SO IMPORTANT ABOUT A STICK?
DON'T TELL ME YOU MASTUR-BATE WITH THIS?
PLEASE DON'T. YOU'LL HURT YOUR-SELF!
THAT'S NOT WHAT IT'S FOR!
ALL RIGHT, SOTA.
RETURN TO NORMAL!
YOU ARE MY...
BROTH-ER!

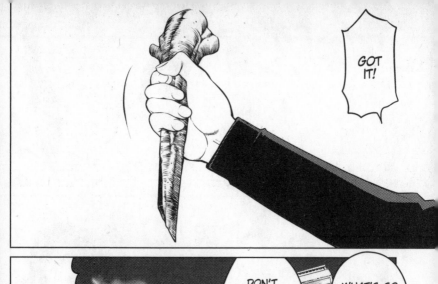

NEE...
CHA--
WH--!
NEE-CHAN, HELP!
A--!
AYANO-SAN KISSED ME!
EEP!
squeeze
squeeze
AAAAAAAAAAARRRRGH!
Oh!
UM... WHAT ARE YOU DOING NOW, KAORU?
I NEED THE STICK!
THE WHAT?

I'M YOUR NEECHAN.
AND YOU'RE MY BABY BROTHER...
SOTA.

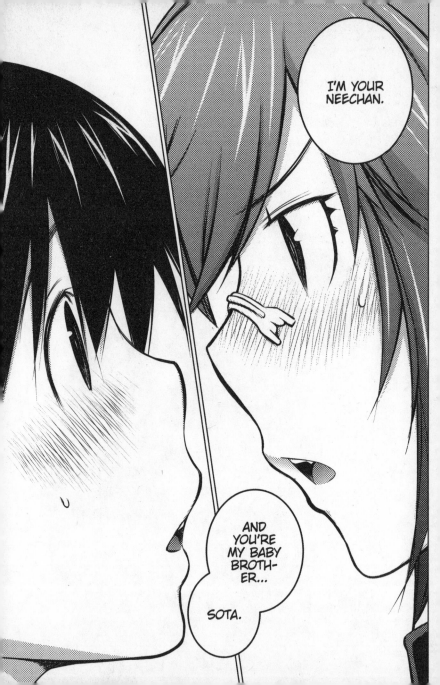

I'LL DO IT...
I'LL KISS HIM...
おおおお...
OOOOOOOW!
MOVE.
AYANO... SAN?

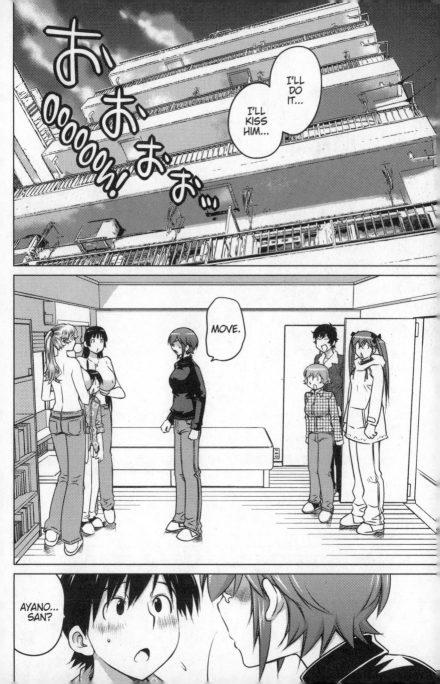

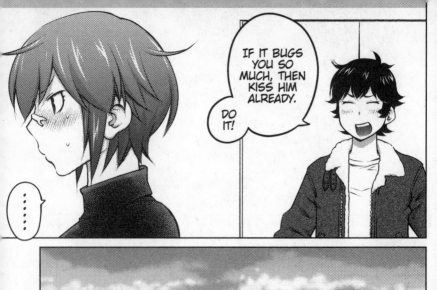

IF IT BUGS YOU SO MUCH, THEN KISS HIM ALREADY.

DO IT!

· · · · ·

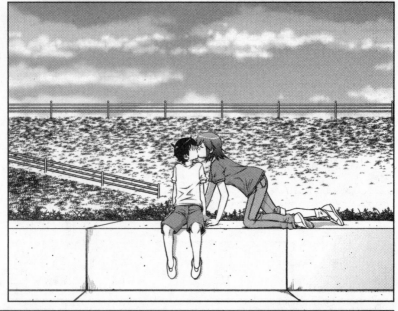

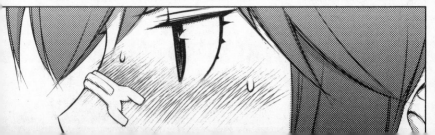

はぁ、Huff!
はぁ、Huff!
Rub スリ
Rub スリ
はぁ、Huff!
はぁ、Huff!
コロ Flop
コロ Flip
SHOCK THERAPY, HUH......?
ALL I SEE IS A BUNCH OF SEX-CRAZED IDIOTS.
WELL, I GUESS THAT'S ONE WAY OF PUTTING IT.

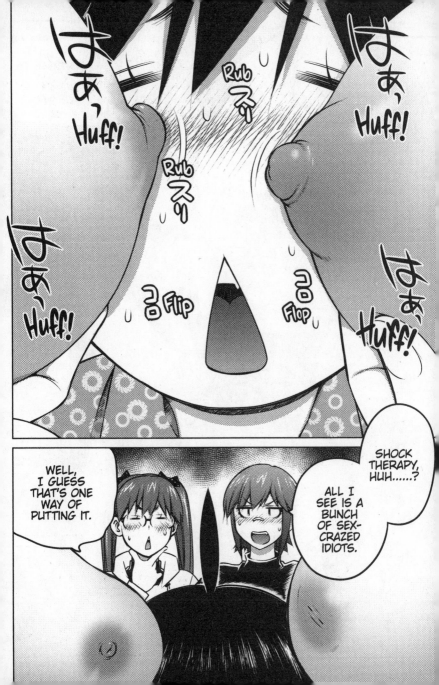

YOUR NEECHAN'S BOOBS ARE HERE FOR YOU.
MINE ARE ONE HUNDRED PERCENT MADE IN THE U.S.A.!
Jiggle ぽよ
Huff! はぁ
Jiggle ぽよ
Jiggle ぽよ
Huff! はぁ
Huff! はぁ
はぁ Huff!

Attack No. 28
Boobie Harem ♥

NO ONE'S PICKED ON SOTA SINCE THAT DAY, AND YET...
KAORU! KAORU!
IT'S THE AMAZON SLUTS AND THEIR TWIN TITS OF TERROR!
I'm your sweet neechan! ♥
ほひぃ…!!
WHEEZE
ほひ…!!
WHEEZE
ワーオ♥
WHEEEEE!
たぷん
Boing
たぷん
Boing
……!!
STOP STANDING AROUND AND DO SOME-THING!

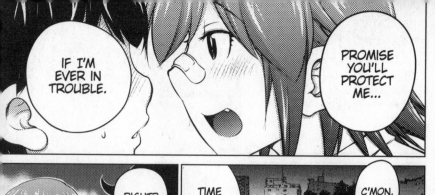

IF I'M EVER IN TROUBLE.

PROMISE YOU'LL PROTECT ME...

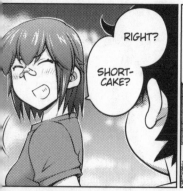

RIGHT?

SHORT-CAKE?

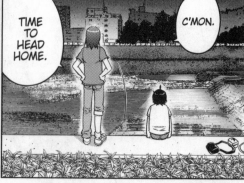

TIME TO HEAD HOME.

C'MON.

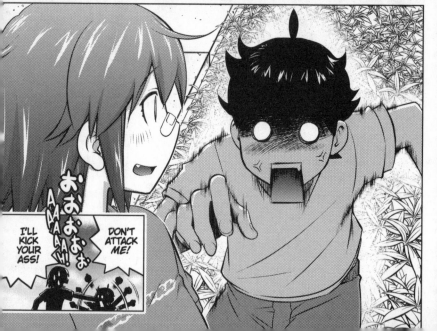

おおおおおおおおおあああああ！！

I'LL KICK YOUR ASS!

DON'T ATTACK ME!

SHORT-CAKE!
QUIT IT.
......
HUH?
THAT'S IT?
I GUESS IT DIDN'T WORK.
OF COURSE NOT.
I'M TOO OLD TO FALL FOR THAT.
IN THAT CASE...
HRM?

OKAY!
GET READY! I'M CASTING THE SPELL!
Shake
......
SWOOOOOSH
HENCE-FORTH, YOU SHALL GO BERSERK WHENEVER ANYONE CALLS YOU "SHORT-CAKE."
A MINDLESS RAMPAGE OF WRATH!
KNOWN AS... BEAST MODE.

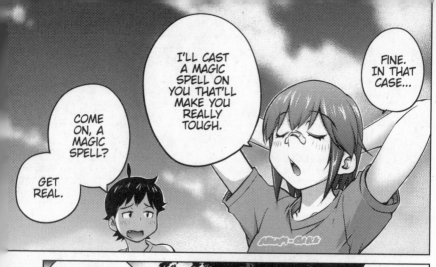

COME ON, A MAGIC SPELL?

GET REAL.

I'LL CAST A MAGIC SPELL ON YOU THAT'LL MAKE YOU REALLY TOUGH.

FINE. IN THAT CASE...

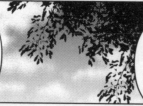

THEY ONLY CALL YOU THAT BECAUSE YOU'RE THE TALLEST GIRL ON THE VOLLEYBALL TEAM.

THEY DON'T CALL ME THE TOYOHIRA WITCH* FOR NOTHING.

JUST LEAVE IT TO YOUR NEECHAN.

*Toyohira is a ward in Sapporo.

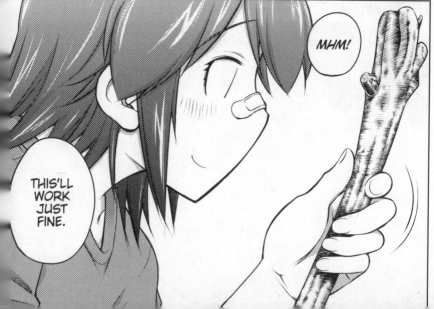

MHM!

THIS'LL WORK JUST FINE.

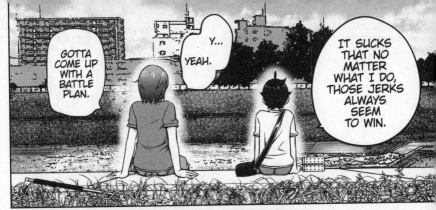

GOTTA COME UP WITH A BATTLE PLAN.

Y... YEAH.

IT SUCKS THAT NO MATTER WHAT I DO, THOSE JERKS ALWAYS SEEM TO WIN.

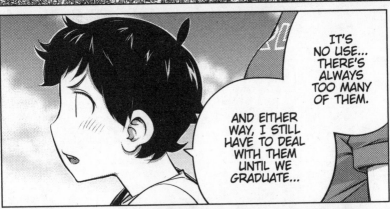

IT'S NO USE... THERE'S ALWAYS TOO MANY OF THEM.

AND EITHER WAY, I STILL HAVE TO DEAL WITH THEM UNTIL WE GRADUATE...

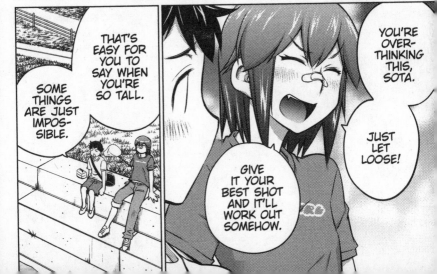

THAT'S EASY FOR YOU TO SAY WHEN YOU'RE SO TALL.

SOME THINGS ARE JUST IMPOSSIBLE.

YOU'RE OVERTHINKING THIS, SOTA.

JUST LET LOOSE!

GIVE IT YOUR BEST SHOT AND IT'LL WORK OUT SOMEHOW.

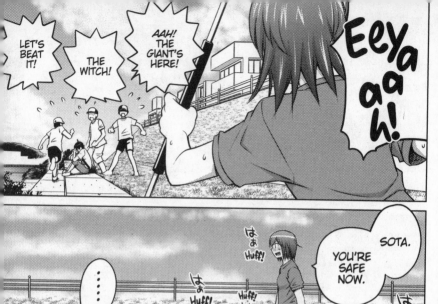

LET'S BEAT IT!

THE WITCH!

AAH! THE GIANT'S HERE!

Eeya aah!

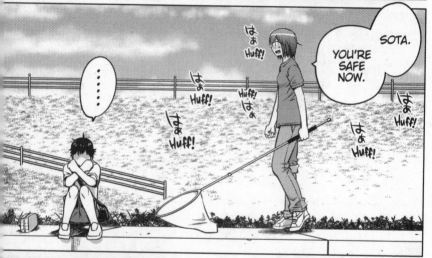

......

SOTA. YOU'RE SAFE NOW.

Huff! Huff! Huff! Huff! Huff!

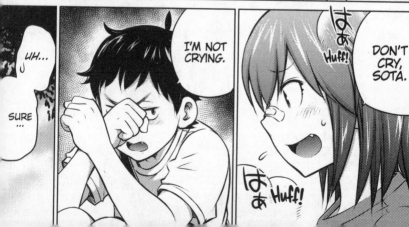

UH...

SURE...

I'M NOT CRYING.

Huff!

DON'T CRY, SOTA.

Huff!

HEY! SQUEAKY!
SHORTCAKE TACHIBANA!
PIP-SQUEAK!
SHORT-CAKE!
SHORTY! SHORTY!
THE TEENIEST WEENIE!
LEAVE HIM ALONE!
YOU STUPID TWERPS!

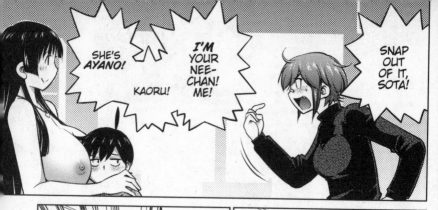

SHE'S *AYANO!*

KAORU!

I'M YOUR NEE-CHAN! ME!

SNAP OUT OF IT, SOTA!

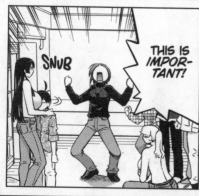

SNUB

THIS IS IMPORT-ANT!

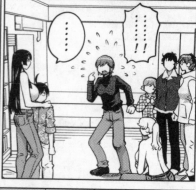

:::

:::!!

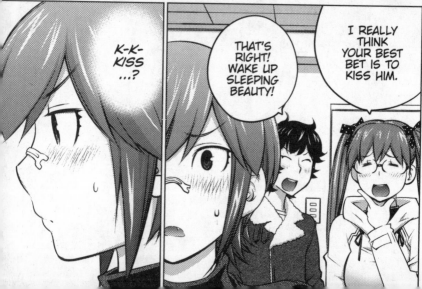

K-K-KISS ...?

THAT'S RIGHT! WAKE UP SLEEPING BEAUTY!

I REALLY THINK YOUR BEST BET IS TO KISS HIM.

HOW...
DO I LOOK?
WOW! A HIGH SCHOOL UNIFORM, HUH?
YOU LOOK GREAT!
SH...
SHUT UP!
WHAT'D I DO?!
Noogie
Noogie
NEE...
CHAN?

NEE...
CHAN...
Shuff
Shuff
Shuff
Shuff
Shuff
Shuff
SOTA!
Shuff
Shuff
Shuff
Shuff
LET'S GO ON A DATE!
Noogie
Noogie

TA-DA!
YOUR NEECHAN'S NAKED BOOBS!
NOT YOU, TOO?!
Arrrgh!
Arrrgh!
ぼいん
Jiggle
C'MON...
KNOCK IT OFF, NEE-CHAN...

Attack No. 27
Sister ☆ Magic

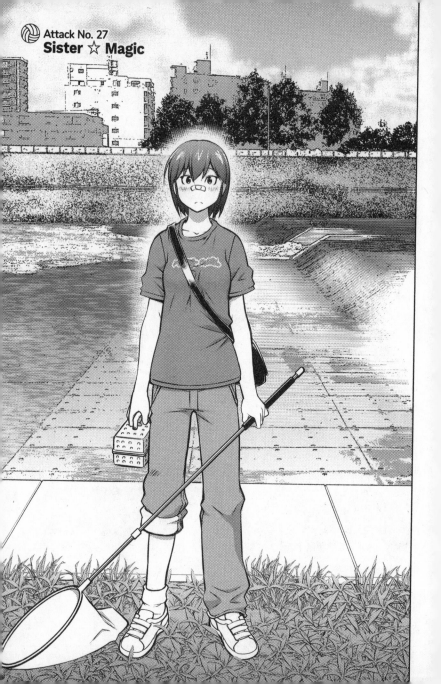

I'M SORRY, AYANO-SAN...
BUT THERE'S ONE THING I WON'T COMPROMISE ON.
WHOOSH
WHEEEE!
BOOBS?!
WHY ARE WE SECOND TO BOOBS?!
Snub
wibble wobble
SLIDE

GRAAAAAA!
ALLOW ME TO EX-PLAIN!
SOTA'S INNER BEAST MODE IS UNLEASHED WHENEVER ANYONE CALLS HIM "SHORTCAKE"!
THUNK
SLUMP
OH...

MAYBE HE NEEDS A STRONGER DOSE.
Brr
Brr
Brr
KISS HIM, KAORU.
LIKE PRINCE CHARMING.
Brr
D--
DON'T BE ABSURD!
Aha!
Poke Poke
HEY THERE.
SHORT-CAKE.
BE A GOOD BOY NOW AND WAKE THE FUCK UP.
SNAP

むにゃ Nyam
THIRTY MORE MIN-UTES...
むにゃ Nyam
HEY!
Hug
Squeeze ぎゅっ
ぎゅっ Squeeze
むふ
Snuggle
NEE-CHAN!
WAIT...
NEE-CHAN ......?

NEE-CHAN!
GET UP!
ガチャ
Ker-Chak
NEECHAN! COME ON!
YOU'RE GONNA BE LATE!
むにゃ
Nyam
FIVE MORE MIN-UTES...
むにゃ
Nyam
MAKE THAT...
SEVEN MORE...
MAYBE TEN...
Lazier by the second.
TIME TO GET THE *HELL* UP!
バッ
Fwip
HEY!

I'M N... NOT TOTALLY ON BOARD, BUT...
はあ Huff!
DO YOU REMEMBER NOW, SOTA? I'M YOUR NEECHAN!
はあ Huff!
Huff! はあ
......
はあ Huff!
はあ Huff!

Snub
HIS BRAIN IS NOTHING BUT BOOBS!
Hey!

ばっ
fling
I KNOW SOTA LOOOVES MOTOR-BOATING BOOBS!
THIS IS THE *BEST* SHOCK THERAPY!
WHAAAT?!
きゃあああ
GYAAAA!
ぽふ Brr
ぽふ Brr
ぽふ Brr
ぽふ Brr
ぽふ Brr
ぽふ Brr
はぁ Huff!
はぁ Huff!
はぁ Huff!
はぁ Huff!
Huff!
Huff!

QUIT IT, AYANO! YOU BIG JERK!
ON THE OTHER HAND, MAYBE--?
ARGH! I DON'T KNOW WHAT TO DO!
Tmp
GRAB
Smoooooch
GYAAAAH!
......
WHAT THE HELL ARE YOU DOING?!
SHOCK THERAPY!
A-AYANO-SAN, DIAL IT BACK...

Y'KNOW...
IT MIGHT BE BETTER FOR EVERYONE IF HIS MIXED-UP MEMORIES STAY THIS WAY.
Gasp!
YEAH!
I'LL HAPPILY PLAY THE PART OF YOUR NEECHAN!
squeeze
WHAAAAT?!
HEY!
Jiggle
WHAAAAT?!

HRM?
ARE YOU OKAY? YOUR CHEEKS ARE BRIGHT RED.
Gasp!
Flinch
U-UM...
IT'S JUST...
AYANO-SAN...
YOU'RE...
THE FIRST GIRL I EVER HAD A CRUSH ON.

LET'S SEE...
WHERE'S THAT PHOTO ALBUM...
THERE'S A VERITABLE SEA OF TROPHIES!
AND NOT ONE CHAMPIONSHIP.
THANKS TO AYANO.
AHA! HERE WE GO!
SOTA! CHECK THIS OUT!
Thwack
SEE?
I'M YOUR NEECHAN!
SHE'S AYANO.
THE ONE WITH THE MONSTER BOOBS.
NOT PULLING ANY PUNCHES, HUH?
Noogie Noogie
Stooop!

WELL, WELL! THE GANG'S ALL HERE.
ぬっ
Hrm?
HEY THERE. COME ON IN.
SOMETHING'S UP, ISN'T IT?
MAKE YOURSELVES AT HOME.
You're all so tall!
You're one to talk!
SORRY FOR BARGING IN!
ARE YOU OKAY, SOTA?
A MOTHER KNOWS!
How sweet!
Here. From everyone.
UH...
I'M FINE.
HOWDY!
SOTA LOOKS JUST LIKE HIS MOM.
SAME WITH KAORU AND HER DAD.
HOW DO YOU KNOW MY HOUSE SO WELL, AYANO-SAN?
OH, YOU KNOW...
I JUST DO.

DAMN IT, SOTA! SNAP OUT OF IT!
I'M KAORU! YOUR BIG SISTER!
Shake Shake
UM...
WHAT ARE YOU TALKING ABOUT, AYANO-SAN?
RRGH ......!
ANYONE HOME?

SHE'S MY SISTER, TACHIBANA KAORU...
AND THIS IS HER NUMBER ONE RIVAL...
HASE-GAWA AYANO-SAN.
WAIT!
SHE'S NOT ...!
IT SEEMS LIKE THE BLOW TO HIS HEAD SCRAMBLED HIS MEMORIES.
NOT MUCH WE CAN DO FOR NOW BUT WAIT AND SEE...

General Hospital
ALL RIGHT, LET'S TRY THIS AGAIN.
TELL ME WHO THESE PEOPLE ARE.
UGH...
LET'S SEE... SHE'S ASAKURA SAKURA, A HUGE ANIME NERD.
Fwip Fwip Fwip Fwip
Ting Ting
AND THE FUNNY ONE!
FLAT-CHESTED TESHIGAWARA KYOKA-SAN.
Knock it off!
JULIA MCKENZIE, THE BASKETBALL STAR.
OUR TEAM CAPTAIN.
AND OUR COACH, HER GAY DAD.
EXCUSE *YOU*! I'M *BI*!
SOME VISIT THIS IS...

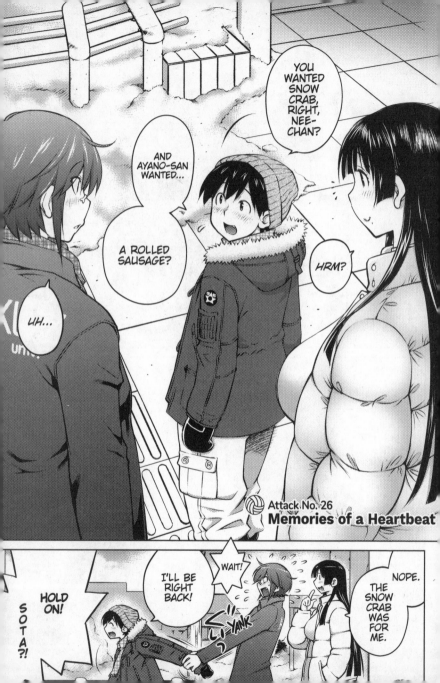

Attack No. 26
Memories of a Heartbeat

THUNK
HEY!
SOTA! ARE YOU OKAY?!
THAT SOUNDED BAD!
GRAB
ARE YOU OKAY?
OOF...
THANKS, NEECHAN.

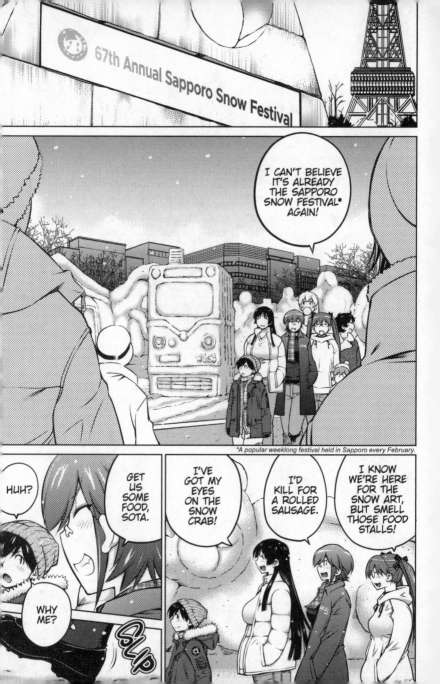

67th Annual Sapporo Snow Festival

I CAN'T BELIEVE IT'S ALREADY THE SAPPORO SNOW FESTIVAL* AGAIN!

*A popular weeklong festival held in Sapporo every February.

HUH?

GET US SOME FOOD, SOTA.

I'VE GOT MY EYES ON THE SNOW CRAB!

I'D KILL FOR A ROLLED SAUSAGE.

I KNOW WE'RE HERE FOR THE SNOW ART, BUT SMELL THOSE FOOD STALLS!

WHY ME?

SLIP

Recap

Tachibana Sota was roped into becoming the coach of his sister's all-girl college volleyball team and the hall director for their dormitory. Being so short and the only boy around, he's naturally the perfect target for these voluptuous amazons' tantalizing teasing and sexual advances. What surprises await Sota as he attempts to navigate the tempting twists and turns of dorm life?

4

Presented By Goro Aizome

C O N T E N T S

*"Play Pig Part II" is a reference to "Playback Part II," a breakup song by Yamaguchi Momoe.

DO YOU LIKE
4
BIG
GIRLS?
story & art by
Goro Aizome